GREAT WALKS FROM WELSH RAILWAYS

**Les Lumsdon
and
Colin Speakman**

SIGMA LEISURE
Wilmslow, United Kingdom

First published in 1989 by
Sigma Leisure, an imprint of
Sigma Press 1 South Oak Lane, Wilmslow, SK9 6AR, England.

British Library Cataloguing in Publication Data

Great Walks from Welsh Railways.
1. Walking - Wales - Guide-books   2. Wales - Description and travel - 1981-
Guide-books
I. Title   II. Speakman, Colin
914.29'04858   DA735

ISBN: 1-85058-104-5

Typeset by Sigma Press

Designed by Kingfisher Design

Cover photograph: Swanlake Bay, near Manorbier.

Acknowledgements: all photographs, including the cover photograph, were kindly provided by the Wales Tourist Board.

FOREWORD

Croeso i Gymru – Welcome to Wales – a walker's paradise with a variety of unspoilt land and seascapes and a host of interesting attractions.

Walking has never been so popular. By using the British Rail network to the full, it still penetrates the rural areas, you can enjoy the countryside and attractions with plenty of time to stand and stare.

Wales has narrow gauge railways too, many linked with main line services. These sturdy trains chug up Snowdon, along the coasts or into the Welsh heartlands - a journey on one or all ten must be part of your visit.

This book highlights many attractions including the beautiful 'Italianate' village of Portmeirion, tranquil Tintern Abbey and the fascinating Llechwedd Slate Caverns. For those preferring solitude, there are halts deep in the countryside especially on the 'Heart of Wales' line.

We offer a warm welcome to all those who love to go a-wandering and I'm happy to join British Rail in introducing you to the very best of Wales.

Prys Edwards,
Chairman,
Wales Tourist Board

THE WALKS – LOCATION MAP

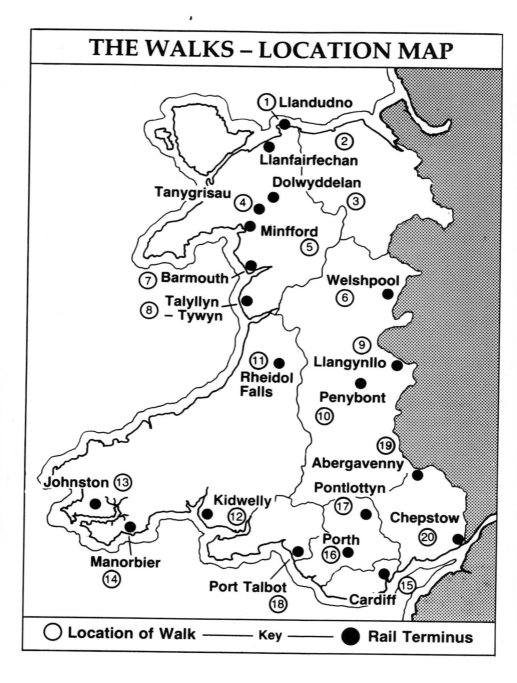

1 Llandudno
2 Llanfairfechan
Dolwyddelan
Tanygrisau
4
3
Minfford
5
7 Barmouth
Welshpool
6
Talyllyn
8 – Tywyn
9
11 Llangynllo
Rheidol
Falls
Penybont
10
19
Abergavenny
Johnston 13
Pontlottyn
Kidwelly
17
12
Chepstow
Porth
20
Manorbier
16
14
15
Port Talbot
18 Cardiff

⊙ Location of Walk ——— Key ——— ● Rail Terminus

CONTENTS

Wales – Land of Mountains and of Railways   7

Some Practical Points   14

THE WALKS

NORTH WALES

1. The Great Orme   18

2. Conwy Mountain   26

3. Lledr and Conwy Valleys   34

4. The Vale of Ffestiniog   41

5. Portmeirion and Criccieth   48

MID WALES

6. Welshpool and Castle Caereinion   57

7. In the Steps of the Drovers –
   Barmouth to Dyffryn   65

8. Talyllyn   72

9. Along Glyndwr's Way 80

10. Llandrindod Wells 86

11. The Vale of Rheidol 92

WEST WALES

12. Cocklers' Ways – Kidwelly to Ferryside 98

13. West Cleddau 104

14. Along the Pembrokeshire Coast 109

SOUTH WALES

15. Three Castles
    – Cardiff, Castell Coch, Caerphilly 115

16. The Rhondda Valley 123

17. Along the Rhymney Ridgeway 129

18. Afan Argoed 135

19. Sugar Loaf 143

20. Tintern Abbey 149

Wales - Land of Mountains and Railways

There can be few small countries in the world that offer so much for the walker as Wales. It's a land of magnificent mountain and coastal scenery, which includes no less than three of Britain's ten National Parks and has a marvellous network of footpaths, bridleways and ancient green ways waiting to be discovered. But unlike so many parts of the world, (Switzerland and Austria being noted exceptions), an excellent public transport system exists to provide access to a great deal, if not all, of the countryside. So you don't always have to worry about a car or taxis to get into many of those wilder places.

A Beauty which is Seductive

Like much of western Britain, Wales has an uncertain climate which means that for quite a few days in the year those magnificent mountain summits are blanketed in mist and rainwear in a rucksack is a necessity. But this is also why the Welsh landscape has such an astonishing greenness, a soft beauty which is as seductive as it is subtle. Unlike the Alpine regions, which can be unbearably hot for serious walking in the summer months, a cool Welsh summer can in fact be perfect walking weather.

But then Wales is somewhere rather special. Many foreigners to Britain, and even many English people, tend to assume that Wales is merely a western chunk of England, as if Middle England had been pushed and squeezed out into that great crescent-shaped piece of land where the spelling is different and people sometimes speak an incomprehensible dialect.

'Cymry'

Nothing can be further from the truth. Britain is, in many ways, a number of very different and distinct peoples and regions. Wales is very much a nation with its own language. This sense of nationhood can be traced back centuries to the Celtic mountain people, those who lived to the west of Offa's Dyke calling themselves *"Cymry"* meaning "comrades" or "compatriots".

Offa's Dyke

Offa's Dyke is the great defensive fortification built in the eighth century by King Offa of Mercia along the historic boundary of Wales to keep the people of Wales out of the rich lands of Saxon Mercia. Not that Offa's Dyke really solved anything, and throughout Norman and Plantagenet times vigorous border disputes flared along the rich and fertile lands known as the Welsh Marches and now forming parts of Clwyd, Cheshire, Powys, Shropshire, Herefordshire, Gloucestershire and Gwent, with a long line of border castles and fortresses being built in what are now busy market towns. Their Norman overlords - Lords of the Marches - were given freedom to plunder deep into Welsh territory.

The Two Llywelyns

It was in the thirteenth century, through the activities of the two Llywelyns, Llywelyn ab Iorwerth, and his grandson Llywelyn ap Gruffydd that Wales began to re-assert her identity. The first Llywelyn, often known as Llywelyn the Great, created an independent state of Gwynedd - the name used for the modern county - over roughly the whole of North Wales except for Montgomeryshire. He established a council of Welsh princes at Aberdyfi and had time to take an interest in English affairs by supporting the English barons who imposed the Magna Carta on King John, and by marrying Joan, John's bastard daughter.

Disputes and civil war after the death of Llywelyn ab Iorwerth were resolved with the emergence of his grandson, Llywelyn ap Gruffydd, as a powerful political leader whom Henry III was forced, in 1276, to acknowledge as Prince of Wales.

Prince of Wales

Llywelyn went on to totally reject all allegiance to the English crown, heading a united Wales, an act of defiance which soon faced the opposition of a much more formidable English ruler - Edward I. After Llywelyn, the last independent Prince of Wales, was slain near Builth in 1282, Edward I completed his conquest by building those massive castles which are still such a feature of the landscape - at Beaumaris,

Conwy, Harlech, Rhuddlan, Flint, Denbigh and above all Caernarfon. It was here that the future Edward II was enthroned as Prince of Wales in 1301. This tradition has been continued ever since.

By now Wales was reduced to becoming little more than a colony of her powerful neighbour - the English establishing new Saxon-style boroughs around their castles, excluding Welshmen from holding land, trading or enjoying civic rights. Yet away from these centres of official power and administration, Welsh life continued. In particular there was a flowering of Welsh literature and poetry in the ancient oral tradition, led by bards attached to the old families.

Owain Glyndwr

Hardship during the 15th century led to a long period of unrest and finally the emergence of another remarkable Welsh Leader - Owain ap Gruffydd, better known as Owain Glyndwr, anglicised to Owen Glendower, the magical rebel leader of Shakespeare's Henry IV. A brilliant political leader as well as a soldier, Glyndwr united his country in rebellion with dissident English nobles against Henry IV, but failed to get sufficient support to overthrow his powerful enemy. Nevertheless, he continued a guerilla campaign against Henry, and was never captured - his death being an unsolved mystery.

Henry Tudor, the grandson of one of Glyndwr's kinsmen, Owen Tudor, became Henry VII and thus founded one of the most glorious English royal dynasties. He also brought "emancipation and liberty" to his fellow countrymen, a process continued by Henry VIII and his Secretary Thomas Cromwell whose Acts of Union of 1536 and 1543 helped to defuse Welsh nationalistic feelings and bring in a long era of peace and prosperity.

The Industrial Revolution

The other great development in Welsh history which has done much to shape the landscape we see and the people we meet today is, of course the Industrial Revolution. Copper, lead, silver and gold mines among the ancient rocks of the North, and in particular the huge expansion of slate quarrying in Snowdonia in the middle of the last century, have left massive scars on the landscape. This is especially so around Blaenau

Ffestiniog where, paradoxically, some surviving mines have been turned into tourist attractions. Welsh slate, carried from the valleys by narrow gauge railway and steam ship, was used for the roofs of buildings throughout Britain and Europe, as well as by generations of children as writing tablets.

The scale of industrialisation in North and Central Wales was nothing compared to that in the South, and most of Wales remains a predominantly rural country, where sheep farming in the hills and dairy farming in the valleys are the dominant land use. Much of the higher land has been used for commercial forestry - a land use not without its fierce critics because of the ecological and social damage resulting from this highly subsidised activity - and also for vast catchment reservoirs supplying water to thirsty industrial cities in the English Midlands.

South Wales

In the South, however, the late 18th century onwards saw the development of the great coalfields. The valleys above Cardiff produced the finest steam coal and anthracite in the world for more than two centuries. When steam engines, rather than diesel or petrol, provided the world's greatest source of mechanised power, and coal rather than oil was black gold, this was highly prized. With the growth of coal mining came the development of iron and steel, with towns like Port Talbot and Merthyr Tydfil growing at a dramatic rate through the 19th century.

Though much of that great heavy industrial base has disappeared through the twin processes of technological and economic change, two thirds of the population of Wales lives in the south, in cities and towns like Cardiff, Swansea and Newport. New industries and activities have come to replace the old. Yet urban and industrial Wales has great beauty too. The industrial valleys are rich in history and in industrial archaeology. They also lie between fine open hills: just to the north lie the Black Mountains and the Brecon Beacons National Park, and - just to the West - the Pembrokeshire Coast National Park.

THE PEOPLE AND A LANGUAGE

An eminent Welsh politician recently suggested that in Wales, as in other parts of Britain, "the landscape is the people". In other words, the landscape that so delights the visitor, the walker in particular, reflects the way of life, culture, and traditions of a community. Destroy that community and you destroy what has made and what can uniquely sustain the landscape. This is especially true of Wales.

It doesn't take the visitor long to begin to notice differences between Wales and England. For one thing, place names on the map are entirely different, and it is well worthwhile learning at least a few common geographic names to assist map reading. For another, in the Snowdonia area in particular you'll meet people in shops, in pubs and on public transport whose first language is Welsh and to whom English is a tongue of strangers.

This is something that English people, whose own language has become so universal, sometimes fail to understand, imagining that it is a deliberate act of rejection. Being able to use your own language to family, friends and fellow countrymen is as important to Welsh people as it is to many other small nations of Europe - a matter of great pride. Hence the need for Welsh on station and road signs, on leaflets and on official documents. Having said that, of course, for many people in South Wales, who haven't grown up in the linguistic communities of the rural North and West, Welsh is a foreign tongue. Yet still a sense of national pride in that language remains.

Not for nothing are Welsh men and women wonderful manipulators of their own and other people's languages. Wales has given the world many gifted writers, orators and politicians. Whatever your views of such diverse political figures as Lloyd George, Nye Bevan or Neil Kinnock, few would deny their gift with words. The Welsh also have a remarkable natural ability for music, encouraged through a great chapel and choral singing tradition which has produced great choirs and great singers throughout the ages.

Welsh people are world famous for their warmth and genuine friendliness. Hospitality is generous, friendly greetings spontaneous. A rambler in Wales will never be short of good company for long.

THE RAILWAYS

The railways of Wales were both a product of and a major contribution to its Industrial Revolution. It was the Great Western Railway, in particular, that came to mean so much to Wales as it spread its tentacles westwards, finally absorbing many other companies on its route to Fishguard. It was the railways which opened up the slate mines of Ffestiniog, in particular the tiny narrow gauge line from Blaenau Ffestiniog to Porthmadog. It was the railways which opened up the massive Rhondda coalfields, served the Ebbw Vale Ironworks, and turned Merthyr Tydfil into one of the world's great iron and steelmaking centres. And it was the railways that brought tourists - the London & North Western line along the North Wales coast to Holyhead for Ireland soon became as important for taking Lancashire and Merseyside holidaymakers to Prestatyn, Rhyl, Colwyn Bay and Llandudno. It was the Cambrian Railways which brought bathers from Birmingham to Barmouth, Pwllheli and the elegant promenades of Aberystwyth. It was the line to Tenby which brought sea and sun seekers from South Wales and from Bristol. It was the Central Wales Line which brought fashionable ladies from Swansea to Llandrindod Wells Spa.

Major Revival as Tourist Routes

Just as in other parts of Britain, the rise of the motor bus and private car brought competition, loss of revenue and, finally, in the Beeching era of the 1960s, swingeing cuts and rail closures. In Wales many lines were closed, but energetic opposition managed to avert closure of several others, most notably the Cambrian Coast and Central Wales Line, both now enjoying a revival as tourist routes. After all, railways have always provided a major encouragement for tourism, and tourism means more money in the local economy. Closing a scenic railway, therefore, is the economic equivalent of shooting yourself in the foot.

Wales has not only led the way in the fight to save and improve the national rail network, but also in the revival and preservation of a number of narrow gauge, private lines. These have been brilliantly marketed as The Great Little Trains of Wales - lines like the Ffestiniog, the Welshpool and Llanfair, the Talyllyn, and the Vale of Rheidol.

These lines - both private and public - are as much part of our heritage, of Welsh history, as the Castles of Edward I or Llywelyn. Nobody has yet suggested that the walls of Conwy Castle should be demolished because they do not pay, yet only a decade ago such a fate was advocated for the Cambrian Coast Line.

This book is about making use of some of these railway lines, not just to enjoy a scenic ride along them, but to actually use them to get into the countryside.

Trains after all have many advantages. They don't pollute, they don't congest, they are a good deal safer than cars, they don't have to be parked. They also happen to be great fun to travel on - a superb way of seeing and enjoying the countryside.

Using The Train

For the walker, trains - and buses - have a special benefit. The walker with a car is attached by that invisible umbilical cord to his vehicle - to which he must always walk back. The train user can alight at one station and walk maybe two, ten or twenty miles before arriving at a little country halt and, perhaps after enjoying appropriate local refreshment, catch the train home. The train user can get deep into the countryside, away from the noise and stench of roads and cars, close to the natural world, a psychological freedom which has to be experienced to be appreciated.

Because Wales has such an excellent network of standard and narrow gauge rail services, and such useful facilities, including bargain tickets, for enjoying them, it's easy to plan a most delightful short holiday there. This book is to help you do just that.

Wales, a beautiful land, awaits you.

Some Practical Points

As in the companion volume, *Twenty Great Walks from British Rail*, we have tried to give the reader the basic essential information for each walk, with starting and finishing stations and points where you can shorten the walk in case of bad weather or other circumstances.

Maps

Remember that neither the description in the text nor the sketch maps are intended to replace good maps, but merely to supplement them. We recommend at very least having the specified magenta-covered Landranger sheets (1:50,000) and preferably the green Pathfinder or yellow Outdoor Leisure (1:25,000) sheets. Pathfinders are amongst the best walkers' maps in the world and no verbal description can replace a good map for accurate information. You'll find the number of recommended maps in the introduction - for Pathfinders the new OS serial number is quoted. However, if one of the excellent and larger Outdoor Leisure Maps is available to cover a particular walk as they are in Snowdonia (these are in effect several Pathfinder sheets integrated to cover the National Park area) these are quoted, as they represent better value for money.

All these walks require some experience of walking in the countryside. If you are a beginner, start with the "easy" routes and work upwards. Estimates of times are only approximate and are based on an average walking speed of around 2mph - but such averages are purely notional and can quickly change in different weather conditions or if there's a lot to see.

Adequate Clothing

Wear decent footwear, which for most of these walks means boots. There is a school of thought which argues for walks in trainers but in certain circumstances and over certain terrain, including many of these walks, they could prove dangerously inadequate. Always carry windproof rainwear, warm outdoor clothing and sufficient food for emergencies - in a rucksack to leave hands free. Compasses should also be carried on upland or moorland walks, and in the darker months take a torch. Leave word with someone where you are going and when you will be expected back.

On every one of these walks please treat the life and work of the Welsh countryside with respect, keeping, whenever possible, to footpaths and taking all litter home with you. "Take only photographs - leave only footprints" is a responsible motto.

Overnight Accommodation

We imagine that most people in this book will be visitors to Wales or visiting a different part of Wales from where they usually live, and so will be staying overnight. You'll find an excellent choice of accommodation, much of it extremely reasonably priced, at or close to the start or finishing points of all these walks. On the other hand you might want to choose a centre in which to stay for a few days and from which you could do three or four of the routes. Barmouth, Llandudno, Aberystwyth, Porthmadog, Machynlleth, Llandrindod Wells, Cardiff or Tenby would all be very suitable for various parts of this book, catching the train in the morning and returning in the evening. This saves the problem and discomfort of having to carry overnight equipment on your back. You'll find the Wales Tourist Board has a wide range of listed accommodation - from simple bed and breakfast establishments, some for £10 or less per night, to farmhouses, inns and hotels - conveniently situated within easy walking distance from railway stations.

Wales has a good network of youth hostels available for the walker. You'll find details in the Y.H.A. handbook; where a Y.H.A. hostel is close or convenient to the start or finish of a walk it is mentioned.

You'll find some useful addresses listed below for enquiries.

There are a number of bargain rail tickets available to cut costs for the walker coming to Wales for a short holiday. As well as the usual Day Return and Saver tickets, there's the British Rail Freedom of Wales ticket covering all B.R. services in Wales for seven days, valid on all rail services after 8.30 a.m. and all day weekends. This is available from B.R. stations or from B.R. Travel Agents in the U.K.

Pass Cambria

Even more flexible for users of this book is the Pass Cambria ticket. This is useable for about two thirds of the walks and is valid on both British Rail and Crosville Wales buses.

Wales Wanderer

There's also a Wales Wanderer Ticket valid on all the narrow gauge lines, but not on B.R. services which limits its value, unfortunately, as far as this book is concerned. Any of the narrow gauge lines including the Talyllyn Railway (address below) will give details.

What you won't find in this book is actual train times, which are likely to change at short notice. These details are available from two sources. The first of these is British Rail's Public Passenger timetable, issued twice a year in May and October, which also contains details of the private Welsh narrow gauge lines. The second is an excellent free pocket-sized publication, the Wales Timetable, published jointly by the Wales Tourist Board and British Rail and consisting of all national and local rail timetables in Wales, both B.R. and narrow gauge.

These details were correct at the time of research but do check fares and service details before travelling.

Principal Rail information Offices in Wales are:

Aberystwyth (0970) 612377	Llandudno Junction (0492) 85151
Bridgend (0656) 57406/7	Neath (0639) 56388
Cardiff (0222) 228000	Newport (Gwent) (0633) 842222
Holyhead (0407) 59222	Port Talbot (0639) 884424
Swansea (0792) 467777	

USEFUL ADDRESSES:

Wales Tourist Board, Brunel House, Fitzalan Road, Cardiff CF2 1UY.
Talyllyn Railway, (Great Little Trains of Wales), Wharf Station, Tywyn, Gwynedd, LL36 9EY. Tel. (0654) 710472.

The Wales Centre, 34 Piccadilly, London W1.

Snowdonia National Park Information Service, Penrhyndeudraeth, Gwynedd, LL48 6LS. Tel. (0766) 770274.

Pembrokeshire Coast National Park, County Offices, Haverfordwest, Dyfed, SA61 1QZ. Tel. (0437) 4591.

The Y.H.A. (Wales) Office, PO Box 7, Cardiff CF2 4XH.

GRADES OF WALKS

"Easy" means that this walk is suitable for people who are not experienced walkers, is fairly level (though there may be uphill stretches) and is likely to be attractive to families with children who are reasonably energetic. "Moderate" assumes that you can cope with longer distances, steeper gradients, slightly more difficult pathfinding and places where the going is a little more difficult. Older children will cope with such routes providing they have had some experience. "Moderately strenuous" or "Strenuous" means that there are stretches of rough going, perhaps steep and boggy places where pathfinding needs some care and skill, particularly when there's a train to catch. For these grades of walk, you must be well equipped, capable of climbing steep or extended hills, used to pathfinding with a compass and perhaps prepared to cross a bit of rough country.

OUR THANKS ....

To British Rail, to the Wales Tourist Board and to the Great Little Trains of Wales for their help support and advice which has proved invaluable. We hope this book will help many more people to discover the opportunities to explore one of the loveliest landscapes in Europe in the most civilised way possible - on foot and by train.

Walk 1: The Great Orme

Landranger Map: Sheet 115.

Pathfinder: Sheet 736 (SH78/98).

Starting Station: Llandudno.

Finishing Station: Deganwy (B.R. Table 83).

Distance: $7^1/2$ miles (12 kms).

Time required: $3^1/2$ hours.

Grade: Easy.

Possible Cut-off point: Haulfre Gardens 5 miles (8 km).

Terrain: Hillside paths and tracks, and foreshore sand-dunes. There is one steepish ascent, to Great Orme Head. This can be avoided by taking the Great Orme Tram (signposted from the town centre), and joining the walk at St Tudno's Church; this saves most of the 650 feet climb and about one mile of the walk.

Refreshment and Accommodation: Ample and a wide choice in Llandudno; choice of shops and cafes in Deganwy. Youth Hostels at Colwyn Bay and Penmaenmawr.

Tourist Information: Chapel Street, Llandudno, Gwynedd, LL30 2SY. (0492) 76413.

THE RAIL JOURNEY

Most people travelling to Llandudno by rail will take either an InterCity service from Crewe and Chester or a Trans-Pennine Sprinter service from Hull, Leeds and Manchester via Chester to Llandudno Junction before changing onto one of the little Pacer trains down the Llandudno branch.

THE WALK

If you're starting the walk coming out of the station, keep directly ahead along Vaughan Street, cross Broadway with its traffic island, and Bodafon Street to the Parade and Promenade, enjoying those lovely shore views. Turn left to follow the Promenade to the Pier, bearing left along the Marine Drive. Cross at the Grand Hotel, looking for a stepped path with a metal handrail almost opposite. Take this pretty zigzag path past sloe bushes and rock roses, to reach a level terrace with views across the elegant Pier. Ahead lie the Happy Valley Gardens.

An Old Copper Mine

These gardens were laid out on the remains of an old copper mine, the Ty Gwyn, which closed down in the 1840s, and were presented to the town by the Mostyn Family to commemorate Queen Victoria's Golden Jubilee in 1887. They now contain botanic gardens rich in rare and tender species of plants and shrubs which flourish in the shelter of the hillside, protected from prevailing winds.

You pass the little open-air theatre which still has traditional seaside concerts, crossing an area of grass where the Gorsedd Circle of Stones used in the 1963 National Eisteddfod held at Bodafon Fields in Llandudno have been erected. Go up the slope beyond the Stones, through a gate into a garden, bearing right and following the path inside the garden steeply uphill. Keep right, under an arbour and along the perimeter fence. Before the stone shelter near the top, look for a little gate right, up limestone steps. This leads to a steep, stepped path which climbs along the large new artificial ski slope served by Llandudno's cable car - and you're likely to have entertaining views of skiers disporting themselves as you climb.

St. Tudno's Church

Your way lies uphill to where the path veers slightly left, now a grassy path between limestone outcrops with magnificent sea views all around you. The path soon descends to follow a wire fence towards a pebble-dashed farm, Penmynydd, where a footpath sign indicates a crossing of paths. Your way is ahead, through the kissing gate to the right of the farm, ignoring the stile on your right. Walk ahead past the farm and through a field gate to reach a broad, grassy track around the farm buildings, soon going alongside fields. Go through the kissing gate ahead onto a lovely enclosed way by hedges and through a second gate before emerging on the lane almost opposite St. Tudno's Church.

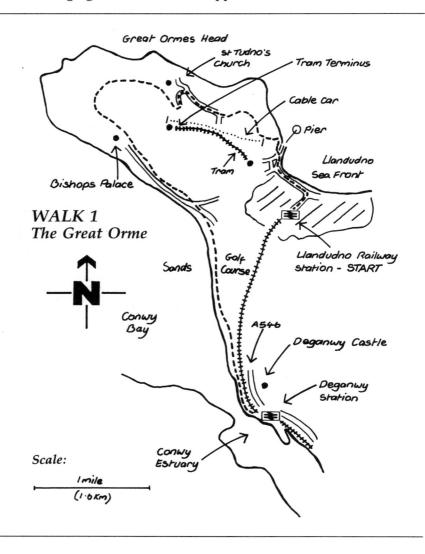

WALK 1
The Great Orme

St. Tudno was a 6th century saint who gave his name to Llandudno; the tiny church dates from medieval times with the north wall of the nave believed to be of 12th or 13th century origin. There is much 15th century work, though the church was largely restored in the 19th century. There is an extensive graveyard and an open air pulpit used in the summer months.

Great Orme Country Park

Turn right to climb the hill past the graveyard, bearing right at the end of the graveyard wall along a very faint path (head for the telegraph poles). You will meet a track by a wall. This is where users of the Tramcar or Cable Car join the route.

Llandudno from the Great Orme

The Serpent

You soon pass the entrance into Great Orme Country Park and Nature Reserve. Follow the track, looking out for a little spring or well set into the wall, said to be of Roman origin. Keep ahead for over half a mile now, through a gate; the stony farm track will soon become a grassy path. Turn left at the wall corner but look for a low mound soon reached on the right. This is a Bronze Age Cairn, probably a burial chamber, and offers a magnificent viewpoint. From it you can see across the vast expanse of the Orme Headland, the name being Viking and meaning the head of a serpent or dragon. On a clear day you can see across the Irish Sea as far as the Lakeland Fells to the north and the Isle of Man to the west, as well as to the peaks of Snowdonia inland.

In the Steps of the Monks

Follow the track left, but after a short way look for a narrow green way (waymarked with a yellow arrow on a rock) which bears steeply right downhill. This is the Monk's Path reputedly used by holy men visiting the ancient Bishop's Palace at Gogarth. According to local folk-lore the soft greenness of the path is a result of the tread of holy feet. True or not, the route is a delight with long views to Llandudno's quieter west shore and on to Deganwy and the Conwy estuary. Follow the way with care as it winds down to join the Marine Drive. The few stones which are all that remains of the Bishop's Palace lie by the foreshore, but are not easily visible from this path.

Go about 100 metres along the Marine Drive, but look for and take a waymarked track left. Keep right at a fork, in front of garages to follow a narrow way behind cottages and garden walls. This soon begins to climb sharply under steep cliffs and craggy outcrops. Luckily there are steps and handrails, but care is needed, before you finally descend to the Toll House at the end of the Marine Drive. The path left here leads into Haulfre Gardens, a pleasant half hour's walk, should you decide to shorten the walk back to Llandudno Station.

Alice in Wonderland

The Golgotha Abbey Hotel was where Mr C. L. Dodgson (1832-98), "Lewis Carroll", visited his good friend Dean Liddell at the Dean's summer family residence. The house was then known as Pen Morfa. He was enchanted by the Dean's daughter, Alice, who became the inspiration for *"Alice in Wonderland"*, the immortal Victorian children's fantasy. It is thought that part of the book may have been written here.

You can see a statue of the White Rabbit from "Alice in Wonderland" as you walk along the west shore, at the end of the Model Yacht pond.

A coastal walk

Continue along the promenade by the sea wall. Where the promenade ends, keep straight ahead past the car park to locate a narrow path that winds along the edge of the sand dunes; the main path bears slightly right to join a stony track which runs along the top of the dunes and gives fine seaward views across the Conwy estuary and to the strange twin humps of The Vadre and Deganwy Castle to your left. Soon the path bears along the edge of the golf course through sand and tussocky grass - avoid walking on the greens.

At the end of the golf course keep the same direction, bearing slightly right to join Deganwy Promenade. Keep ahead for the level crossing and the little station. There are frequent trains back to Llandudno or forward to the Junction. If there's time, visit the ruins of the Castle on The Vadre, rich in Welsh history, which has such a strategic position guarding the Conwy Estuary.

Deganwy Castle

Deganwy castle was where the kings of the ancient Kingdom of Gwynedd held court in the Fifth and Sixth Centuries, including King Maelgwyn, reputedly an unstable, unruly character who ruled the whole of Wales from here between 530 and 540 A.D. It is thought the first ever Welsh Eisteddfod was held at The Vadre in medieval times, but the Castle's colourful history came to an abrupt end in 1263 when it was demolished by Llywelyn ap Griffydd to keep it out of the hands of the English. This led Edward I to choose Conwy, rather than Deganwy, as the site of his main fortress to guard the important Conwy estuary.

To visit the Castle ruins, take the Llandudno road, turning right past the shops into York Road. At the top of the road, where it curves right, a fieldpath leads to the foundations of the Castle, between the twin hummocks of the hill. A fine viewpoint across the tiny peninsula makes up for the lack of much to see.

Walk 2: Conwy Mountain

Landranger Map: Sheet 115.

Pathfinder: Sheets 736,752, (SH77/78).

Outdoor Leisure (part): Sheet 16 (Conwy Valley Area).

Starting Station: Llanfairfechan.

Finishing Station: Conwy (B.R. Table 83).

Distance: 11 miles (17 kms).

Time required: $5^1/2$ hours.

Grade: Moderate.

Terrain: Tracks and open hill paths; two steepish sections.

Possible Cut-off point: Penmaenmawr 7 miles (11 kms).

Refreshment and Accommodation: Good facilities available at both Llanfairfechan and Conwy. Refreshments available in summer at Ty'n-y-ffrith farm (6 miles). Youth Hostels at Bangor, Paenmaenmawr and Rowen.

Tourist Information: Castle Street, Conwy, Gwynedd LL32 8AY. Tel. (0942) 592248.

THE RAIL JOURNEY

Between Llandudno Junction and Bangor, the North Wales Coast Line skirts the edge of the Snowdonia National Park. It crosses the Conwy Estuary through Robert Stephenson's fine tubular railway bridge built 1846-8, and the new Conwy station lies under the castle walls. It then follows the narrow ledge beneath Conwy Mountain and Penmaen Bach

26

along Conwy Bay, reaching the little quarry town of Penmaenmawr, dominated by the massive partially quarried summit of Penmaenmawr mountain.

Lavan Sands

Skirting the coast to Llanfairfechan the railway passes the great sandbanks of Lavan Sands, with views across to Anglesey before swinging past Penrhyn Castle and its park into the University town of Bangor. Ahead lies a journey across the Britannia Bridge, also built by Robert Stephenson and opened in 1850, across the spectacular Menai Straits, past the most memorably named station at Llanfairpwllgwyn-gyllgogerychwyrndrobwyll llantysiliogogogoch and across the green expanse of Anglesey to Holyhead for the Irish ferries.

THE WALK

This is a particularily impressive walk offering superb mountain and coastal scenery even though the walking is not strenuous.

From the entrance of the little unstaffed halt at Llanfairfechan, turn left into the station drive, and right at the road junction into the town centre, where you have a choice of shops, pubs and cafes. Cross the main A65 at the traffic lights, and keep along the road directly opposite. At a fork where the road to the right is signed to the Town Hall, keep left by a garage, along Park Road, following the road as it curves round to the left.

Anglesey Views

This road goes through suburban housing before ending at a gate into a park marked "Private - please shut the gate". It is in fact a public path through Penmaen Park, a stretch of lovely open parkland, with superb views across the coastline, to the tip of Anglesey and Puffin Island.

At the end of the parkland go through a gate and into a lane past houses, descending slightly. Keep ahead to where the lane bends sharply left in front of a house. Your way is to the right up a narrow,

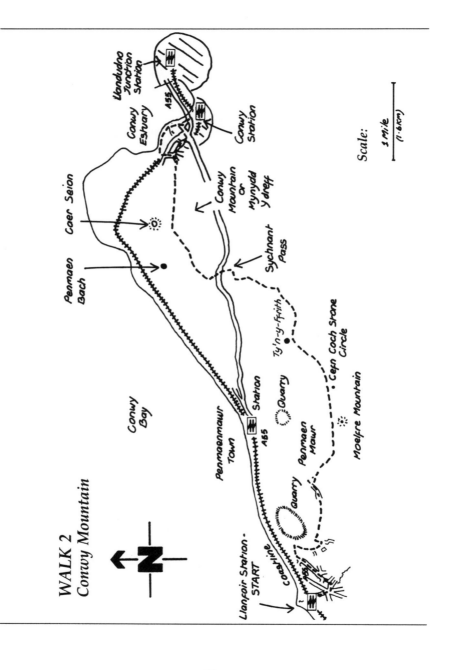

WALK 2
Conwy Mountain

N

Scale:
1 mile
(1.6km)

grassy way to a crossing of paths. Your way is the narrow path to the right, which soon zigzags sharply uphill, climbing through a lovely old coppice by a wall. This now becomes a sunken way through elms, ashes, oaks and sycamores, going through a gate and between stone walls, with fine views across to the Menai Straits and, in the distance, Beaumaris Castle on Anglesey.

At Henar Farm fork left through a gate along the fence uphill to another gate; where the main path swings left in a wood, go through the a kissing gate in the bend. The path continues in the same direction uphill, alongside a wall. Head for a gap in the field wall ahead, then bear left uphill towards farm buildings above. There are superb views all around you as you ascend.

The path goes through gates between the farm buildings before going right near the farm then left onto a grassy track, signed, and on to another gate. It now enters a stretch of open moorland; some careful map reading is required here. Follow the path up to a group of oak trees before picking up the line of sunken sled tracks which soon bear sharply right through the heather and climb steeply up the hillside, with ever more splendid views to compensate for the hard work.

Behind Penmaenmawr

You soon reach a kissing gate ahead in a wall. The path now follows the wall almost due eastwards, above the enclosures. Keep ahead until you join the quarry road.

Turn right here, climbing uphill for around 300 metres. Before the warning notices for the quarry, (informing you that it is dangerous to proceed between 1200-1230 on Mondays to Fridays and 1100 - 1140 on Saturdays), turn right onto a green way over open moorland. Keep the wall to your right.

You are now walking along the back of Penmaenmawr mountain and onto a long green ridge with ever more open views of the outlying ranges of Snowdonia to your right. Near a sheepfold the ways split, one track following the wall round to the right, the other, the fainter way, continuing straight ahead along the shoulder of Dinas Penmaen, a steep little summit to your left. Keep ahead, the path bearing left until it joins a broader, stony track which climbs up the valley to the left and along the side of Moelfre hill to the right.

As you proceed, you will enjoy, if the weather is clear, ever more splendid views, particularily through the gap between Penmaenmawr and Conwy Mountain, across Conwy Bay. Here the huge brooding limestone form of the Great Orme looks almost like an island attached to the mainland by the narrow, sandy peninsula on which the town of Llandudno stands.

Stone Circle

Ahead you will see a stone circle, strategically placed on a headland known as Cefn Coch. The fine green way climbs up to the left of it. It is worth leaving the path as it crosses a dip to enjoy the site of the strange circle of stones refered to on some maps as a "Druid's Circle" but more likely to be of Bronze Age origin. Whatever its history, this is another fine viewpoint of sea and mountains.

Return to the track, keeping ahead past a footpath sign and then bearing left until the red roofs of a farm called Bryn Derwydd come into view. Before reaching the farm follow the path sharp right through a gate, then left alongside a fieldwall, past the front of the farm. Keep ahead through gates along the farm track, but just before a junction of paths a narrow link path will take you down to Ty'n-y-ffrith, a farm and group of cottages which has a welcoming tea garden in the summer months.

Across the Sychnant Pass

The route continues along the green way past the cottages. Bear left as its swings right at a fork onto a narrow path which becomes a green way through the bracken by a wall. Should weather or fatigue have persuaded you to end the walk here, there is a direct track from here down to Conwy Old Road for Penmaenmawr station - about 2 miles away.

Otherwise, cross the metal stile in the wall, left - made out of old mine railway lines - and descend to a stile and a stream crossing. Cross here and follow the path alongside the wall - but take care to avoid some muddy ground after wet weather. Keep ahead under pylons to join a clearer, stony track running along a low ridge above. At a junction of paths bear left along a well made path. Where this swings right look for a stile in the wall. This crosses to a grassy track through the heather at the side of the hill known as Maen Esgon. Keep on this clear track, as it winds round through the heather in a long "S" shape which eventually curves round into a grassy hollow. Keep left at the next junction of paths towards a little wooded crag ahead, around and to the left of which the path winds before joining a path from the right which leads to the road at the top of the Sychnant Pass.

This is a very dramatic point where the old road - once the main coach road from Conwy to Bangor before the turnpike road around the coast was built - climbs a murderously steep gradient, with views down the green valley of Dwygyfylchi to the coastal road and railway.

Conwy Mountain

Your way lies on the track directly opposite which contours around the hillside above the lip of the pass, again with fine views below. Bear right with the path until the end of the wall by Allt-Wen hill. Stay on the track at a fork, bearing right, uphill; go right at the next junction; then bear left along a narrow way which climbs steeply through the heather up the great ridge of Conwy Mountain to your left. Make your way to the top of the ridge with its vistas across Conwy Estuary, to Deganwy, Llandudno and the Orme, and a dizzy descent to the coast road below, where cars look like toys.

Though only 809 feet above sea level, this is a thrilling viewpoint and a fitting climax to a walk where, if weather conditions are clear, panoramic views of mountains and coast are to be enjoyed in abundance. Nor is the summit without historic interest. At Caer Seion, just below the summit cairn, lie the remains of a pre-Roman, presumably Iron Age, hillfort.

Into Conwy town

The descent, because it is so steep, requires a little care, but views across the rooftops of this little walled town are ample compensation. The paths converge steeply down the breast of the mountain, finally emerging in a narrow way behind a walled estate and finally by cottage gardens into a lane. At a junction into a broader lane, turn left to reach the railway crossed by a narrow bridge. Keep ahead to a crossing over the busy road and continue along Morfa Drive, past a school. At the end of Morfa Drive a path bears right to lead by the medieval town wall to the quayside of this most picturesque of little harbours. Here you will still find an odd fishing boat between the pleasure craft and the nation's smallest house reputedly hides among other quayside features. Cobbled ways lead into the town.

Conwy Castle and Estuary

Conwy

Conwy is a town to savour. Its magnificent castle was built between 1283 and 1289 by Edward I as part of his grand strategy to subdue the Welsh. With its beautifully proportioned towers and its majestic great hall it is one of the finest medieval fortifications in Western Europe. Time your walk to enjoy a visit. There's also the 16th century Plas Mawr house, now a museum; the Old Toll House; the town walls; Thomas Telford's elegant suspension bridge, built for Irish Mail coaches, but now reserved for pedestrians; a Heritage Centre; and a good choice of friendly pubs and cafes.

You'll find Conwy's little railway station at the top of the town. It was reopened as recently as 1987, after being carefully rebuilt in sympathetic materials to blend in with the nearby castle and town walls, and is an excellent way of bringing people to and taking them from Conwy without adding to traffic and parking problems. There's a frequent train service to Llandudno Junction, Chester and Bangor whenever you can manage to drag yourself away from the town's many attractions.

Walk 3: Lledr and Conwy Valleys

Landranger: Sheet 115.

Outdoor Leisure Map: Sheet 16 Snowdonia - Conwy Valley.

Starting Station: Dolwyddelan.

Finishing Station: Betws-y-Coed (B.R. Table 84).

Distance: 8 miles (13 km).

Time Required: 5-6 hours.

Grade: Moderate - but with one substantial climb.

Possible Cut-off point: No suitable point.

Terrain: Mainly tracks across mountainous country with narrow paths alongside Afon Llugwy.

Refreshment and Accommodation: Dolwyddelan offers accommodation and refreshment and there is a youth hostel at nearby Pont-y-Pant. There is a plentiful supply of accommodation at Betws-y-Coed.

Tourist Information: Royal Oak Stables, Betws-y-Coed, Gwynedd, LL24 0AH. Tel. (06902) 426/665.

THE RAIL JOURNEY

The Conwy Valley line, which runs for 28 miles from Llandudno Junction to Blaenau Ffestiniog, is scenically magnificent. It begins in the Conwy estuary, opposite Conwy Castle itself, and follows Afon Conwy deep into the heart of the Snowdonia National Park. Initially, the line goes past marshes and mud flats where you're likely to see a heron lazily flapping its way across the river as the train approaches. The little station at Tal-y-Cafn was once the site of the main ferry across the estuary, and from here it is only a short walk to the magnificent gardens at Bodnant (open to the public daily thoughout the summer). Gradually, as the hills get steeper, the valley narrows until at Llanrwst river, road and railway share the narrow valley floor.

The Lledr Valley

Beyond Betwys-y-Coed the little single track line begins to twist its way through woodland and deep cuttings into the narrow Lledr Valley. There are sudden views of mountain summits as you emerge into the open, past the little halts at Pont y Pant, Dolwyddelan and Roman Bridge, before plunging into the 2 mile tunnel under Moel Dyrnogydd which emerges into the slate landscapes of Blaenau Ffestiniog. This is where the Conwy Valley line links with the Ffestiniog narrow gauge railway (see Walk Four).

Gwynedd County Council sponsors a Sunday train service along the line during the summer months - The Sunday Shuttle. Look out for leaflets. If you are doing this walk from Dolwyddelan, don't forget to inform the guard as you board the train, as this is a request stop.

Dolwyddelan

The name Dolwyddelan derives from the word "Dol" for meadow and the name of "Gwyddeln" who was a 6th century Welsh saint. The castle, on a steep ridge west of the village, dates from the late 12th century and was probably built by a local prince, Iorwerth Trwyndwn - known as "the flat nosed". The castle is traditionally reputed to have been the birthplace of Llywelyn the Great, Prince of Wales. It was attacked and captured by Edward I in 1283. The castle ruins are open daily, admission free.

The present village of Dolwyddelan is an attractive settlement along the A670 with shops, cafes, a pub and a medieval church, a useful starting point for a number of forest and mountain walks.

THE WALK

From Dolwyddelan railway station gateway, turn left and then go right over the bridge crossing the Afon Lledr towards the village. After approximately 200 metres take the paved footpath right, across the field opposite the church. When you reach the the main A470 road cross and turn right. Walk for a short distance then bear left into a lane signed to Capel Curig. This lane immediately climbs very steeply, winding between a number of houses. Ignore the turning to the left and continue ahead up a little pass, Allt Singrug. The track climbs up to join another track. Bear right here.

Across Clogwyn-llwyd

Pass through the Forestry Commission gate and turn left onto a track ahead. Foel Gynnud stands to your right and there are impressive views of the Lledr valley below. Continue through the forest, ignoring a path to the left, but at the next junction follow the main track bearing left. Avoid turnings to the left and right as you proceed to the summit, some 860 feet above sea level. Your track descends now and you cross a stream, Afon Ystumiau, still ignoring tracks off to the left and right.

You come to another crossroads. Follow the track bearing to the right and continue ahead. Another track soon joins from the left. The track forks again and you take the right hand fork which leads to a gate at the edge of the forest near Clogwyn-llwyd - Grey Crag. A slightly sunken and worn track leads across the moorland with, if it is clear, views across to the craggy summit of Moel Siabod (2,861 feet, 872 metres) and beyond to the giant peaks of Snowdonia.

Cross a stile beside a gate and continue ahead, the track now being walled on one side and fenced on the other. The track turns left through the wall and runs parallel to the original route. The Llugwy valley now comes into view with a marvellous mountainous panorama beyond.

After a short distance another track crosses but you continue downhill, the track bearing slightly left now. It proceeds to wind quite steeply and you come to a stile. Cross it and turn right into a tarmac lane. Follow this quiet lane for about one mile until it reaches the the main A5 road. Turn left to cross the road bridge. Cross the road.

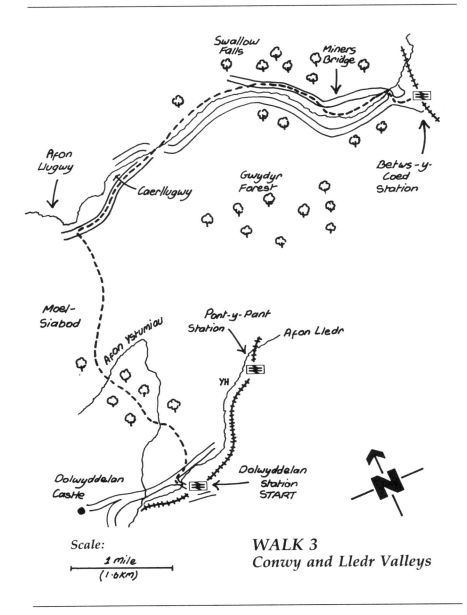

Swallow
Falls

Miners
Bridge

Afon
Llugwy

Caerllugwy

Gwydyr
Forest

Betws-y-
Coed
Station

Betws-y-Coed Station

Moel-
Siabod

Afon Ystumiau

Pont-y-Pant
Station

Afon Lledr

YH

Dolwyddelan
Castle

Dolwyddelan
Station
START

N

Scale:

1 mile

(1·6km)

WALK 3
Conwy and Lledr Valleys

Ty-hyll

The little house on the corner is Ty-hyll, the "ugly house" a little traditional Welsh house built of water smoothed river cobbles. It is open to the public on most days for a small charge.

Your way is down the steps to the right at the end of the bridge. Follow the clear path by the River Llugwy - a delightful riverside walk.

Swallow Falls and the Miners' Bridge

This path eventually reaches Swallow Falls. The section at the Falls is badly eroded by the feet of thousands of visitors and you may have to follow a diversion. But the views back across these spectacular falls, the peaty brown waters turning creamy white as they split round stones, are worth the effort. The Swallow Falls may be a cliché but like many attractions everyone knows about there is very good reason for their fame. The falls are particularly thrilling after wet weather.

Once past the Falls ignore the track bearing to the left but follow the path downhill and straight ahead. Some of the steeper sections are eroded, so care is required. Ford a stream by stepping stones and follow the path through the woods. Cross another small stream and the path now becomes a rough forestry track. Climb up through a wood graced by mature trees and then follow the track down to join a tarmac lane. Bear right here.

Follow the lane through deep forest for about half a mile. As it begins to bend more sharply to the left a path drops down to the river to the Miners' Bridge - an extraodinary steep little wooden bridge over the river, originally built, as the name implies, for local lead miners. Below the bridge is a series of smaller falls. You might wish to wander across to enjoy them more fully - perhaps for a photograph. If you do so, take care over the smooth and treacherously slippery stones around the riverside.

The route continues back across Miners' Bridge by the riverside path which continues downstream, close to the river. This is a popular, probably over-used path and is easy to follow along the banks of the Llugwy before rejoining the lane once again.

Keep right as the lane drops by a car park into Betws-y-Coed. Turn left to the centre of the town and the railway station.

Betws-y-Coed

Betws-y-Coed, Snowdonia's most popular tourist centre, is an old coaching town on the London-Holyhead road at the centre of three valleys - the Conwy, Lledr and Llugwy. It has a number of hotels that catered for the coach and train tourists of the last century, and has expanded to cater for the motorised visitors of the present. There are shops, cafes and pubs, including the larger type of souvenir shop, outdoor shops and craft centres and the inevitable large coach parks for more sedentary travellers.

Snowdon and Lynau Mymbyr

You can explore such tourist spots as The Fairy Glen and Conwy Falls, which are only a short walk from the town. There's a National Park Centre with an exhibition about local geology, natural history and agriculture which includes a talking farmer - or at least an animated

39

model! Even the little station boasts a cafe, a hairdresser and a small railway museum which you can enjoy before catching the train which whisks you back by the quieter delights of the Conwy Valley Line.

over a stream, then sharply right up an extremely steep ravine alongside the stream. Take your time climbing up here; you will soon see the railway line. The path finally joins a crossing path leading to a pretty waterfall to the right - an ideal place to rest and recover from the climb in the evocatively named Coed-y-Bleiddiau, "the wood of the wolves".

Llyn Mair

Retrace your steps to the top of the ravine, this time continuing below and parallel to the railway line along a path (not shown on the map but a well used route, recently improved) between railway and forest fence. This eventually broadens into a forestry track, gradually descending to reach, after about half a mile, a gate at the main B 4420 road opposite the end of a small lake, Llyn Mair.

Turn left along the road, but at the end of the lake look for a stile, right, leading into the middle of a Nature Trail. Keep right at a junction of tracks (Point 9 on the trail) around the edge of the lake, eventually climbing into the woods again below the railway. Keep straight ahead where the path bends left to join a broader track swinging right. Bear right at the next junction going round the lake to emerge, over a wooden bridge, at the lake shore car park on the main road where there are delightful lakeside views.

Almost directly opposite, on the far side of the road, you'll find a stepped path climbing uphill. Cross a stile and bear left by a stream climbing up to the railway. Close to the line look for the way left, crossing the stream, which brings you along the railway and into the little station of Tan-y-Bwlch. Here you will find refreshments, souvenir shop and comfortable facilities, as well as, in the main season at least, frequent services to Porthmadog or Blaenau Ffestiniog.

Walk 5: Portmeirion and Criccieth

Landranger Map: Sheet 124.

Outdoor Leisure Map: Sheet 18 Snowdonia (Harlech & Bala).

Starting Station: Minfford (B.R. or F.R.).

Finishing Station: Criccieth (B.R. Table 76).

Distance: 12 miles (20 km) This does not include any walking in the Portmeirion estate.

Time required: 6 hours.

Grade: Moderate.

Possible Cut-off point: Porthmadog 6 miles (10km).

Terrain: Woodland tracks and paths in the initial stages, then sand dunes and beach.

Refreshment and Accommodation: Cafes, Restaurants in Portmeirion; excellent choice of cafes, pubs, and overnight accommodation in Porthmadog; cafe in Borth-y-Gest; wide choice of cafes, pubs in Criccieth. The nearest Youth Hostel is at Harlech.

Tourist Information: High Street, Porthmadog, Gwynedd, LL49 9LP. Tel. (0766) 512981.

THE RAIL JOURNEY

In a land so richly endowed with scenically beautiful railways as Wales, the Cambrian Coast Railway is perhaps the finest. The 58 miles from Machynlleth Station to Pwllheli passes coastal, estuarine and mountain scenery without equal south of the Scottish border. Built between 1863 and 1867 by the Cambrian Railways (which was not absorbed into the Great Western Railway until 1923) it opened up this part of the coast for slate, fishing and the holiday resorts which were soon to be established. Its stations have been restored in the handsome mid green and white colours of the Cambrian Railways.

Dovey Junction

The single track route leaves the main Cambrian Line (Aberystwyth route) at Dovey Junction to follow the Dovey Estuary around the great headland which forms the perimeter of the Snowdonia National Park to Aberdyfi before turning northwards, along the edge of Cardigan Bay. Still clinging to the coast, the line reaches Tywyn, terminus of the narrow gauge Talyllyn Railway (see Walk 20), the first preserved line in Wales, before going along a breathtaking narrow rocky shelf above cliffs by Llangelynin and Llwyngwril. This stretch of line contains Britain's only avalanche shelter protecting the line from rockfall to prevent the kind of terrible disasters that were suffered here because of rock falls in 1883 and 1933.

The Barmouth Bridge

Once past Fairbourne, the junction for yet another narrow gauge railway, comes one of the most famous features of the line, the Barmouth Viaduct. This magnificent viaduct across the Mawddach Estuary, half a mile long and made of timber, had to be closed to traffic in 1980 owing to damage by marine worms, and was only reopened for lightweight railcars in 1981. Major reconstruction work completed in 1986 enabled locomotive-hauled trains to run once again into the seaside resort of Barmouth, including the "Snowdonian" express direct from London Euston. In the summer months steam locomotives are to be seen hauling the Cambrian Coast Express from Machynlleth - a magnificent sight as they cross Barmouth Bridge.

Harlech Castle

The scenery is a little less dramatic from Barmouth northwards as the line follows a narrow coastal lowland strip and you are soon under the very walls of Harlech Castle. The line then swings around the great estuary formed by the rivers Afon Dwyryd and Afon Glaslyn, as they come into Porthmadog Bay. The line goes under the older Ffestiniog railway viaduct into Porthmadog, then swings westwards along the beautiful Lleyn Peninsula to Criccieth. It passes the remains of Afon Wen station, once the main junction with the London and North Western Railway railway to Caernarfon and Bangor, before it reaches Pwllheli, the main market town for the area and a popular holiday resort.

THE WALK

You can start this walk at Minfford Station either from the Cambrian Coast Line, or from the adjacent Ffestiniog Railway whose station platforms you pass on the exit under the tunnel and up the steps from the British Rail line.

Portmeirion

Turn right outside the station along the main A487 towards the centre of the village, keeping to the same side of the busy main road. Cross at the pedestrian crossing, then turn left at the first junction, signed Portmeirion. Where the main drive signed to Portmeirion goes off sharp right, look for a parallel track, which starts opposite the telephone box, running behind gardens. This is a quieter,traffic free way which soon diverges from the road through woodland. At a fork take the lower path by Cae Canol, an attractive green way which eventually rejoins the busy drive into Portmeirion by hydrangeas. Keep ahead along this drive as it curves to the car park and main entrance to Portmeirion.

This remarkable Italianate village, open to the public between April and October, is something unique in the British Isles. A delightful "folly" in the 18th century sense of the word, it was largely the creation of one man, the late Sir Clough Williams-Ellis, architect, who bought what was a typical small Welsh country estate in 1925, and, inspired by Portofino in Italy, renamed it Portmeirion. Over the next half century he filled it with an astonishing range of buildings and gardens in the style of baroque Italy and Austria - and almost everything else that took Sir Clough's eclectic fancy.

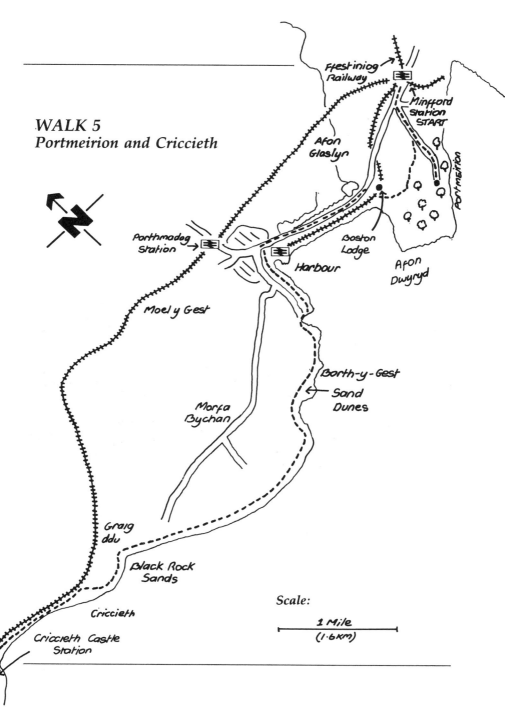

WALK 5
Portmeirion and Criccieth

Ffestiniog Railway

Minffordd Station START

Afon Glaslyn

Portmeirion

Porthmadog Station

Boston Lodge

Harbour

Afon Dwyryd

Moel y Gest

Borth-y-Gest
Sand Dunes

Morfa Bychan

Graig ddu

Black Rock Sands

Criccieth

Criccieth Castle Station

Scale:

1 Mile
(1·6km)

51

Portmeirion now flourishes as a major tourist attraction. It is well worth exploring, not only for the central core of the village itself, with its cafes and restaurants, hotel, pottery, craft and book shops, but also for the superb semi-natural woodlands and coastal paths, a kind of semi official country park with superb views across the estuary.

Portmeirion 'Italianate' Village

Entrance to Portmeirion is fairly expensive (this is a private estate), but the charges help to finance the upkeep of this fine estate. Allow at least two hours to explore the village, gardens and the woods, and if you are so entranced by what you find that there isn't time to complete the full walk, you can always end your journey at Porthmadog.

Across The Cob

The easiest way to leave the estate without complications of trespass is to follow the main one way system for cars along the metalled drive up out of the woods past Castelldeudraeth, which eventually rejoins the entrance drive. Soon after this, look on the left for a grassy track, signposted, which climbs through and follows the top of a wood, through gates and by a wall to a crossroads. The house of Plas Penrhyn, just visible on the right, was the home of Bertrand Russell, the great philosopher and peace campaigner.

Keep directly ahead at the crossing tracks along a stony track which ascends a knoll. At a farm go straight through the farm gate. The path, signed, turns right at the bottom of a field. There are superb views from here across the estuary and Tremadog Bay. Go through another gate, following a fence and soon bearing right onto a lovely grassy path, which looks very much like an engineered quarry track or old railway. There are views over The Cob through the oak trees.

This path emerges at Boston Lodge Halt and engineering works on the Ffestiniog Railway, at the end of which steps lead to the main road. Keep on the same side of the road, close to the wall to avoid the traffic past the toll gate (pedestrians free) to reach the steps up onto the Cob.

The Cob was built between 1808 and 1811, originally part of a major scheme by another remarkable Welshman, W. A. Madocks to drain and reclaim the marsh and mudflat land of Traeth Mawr. The settlements of Tremadoc and the once important slate port of Porthmadog were named after him. At first the road went across the top of The Cob, but when the railway was opened in 1836 to bring Ffestiniog slate down to the new port for shipment to other parts of Britain and overseas, the road was shifted to its present position. The path runs alongside the railway and you may be lucky enough to share your one mile journey to Porthmadog harbour with one of the little steam engines now carrying its load of tourists, not slates, across the Bay.

Porthmadog

You emerge in the centre of Porthmadog, close to the harbour. Take time not only to enjoy some well earned refreshment, but also to visit two extremely interesting little museums here. The first of these is that of the Ffestiniog Railway in the station which has a number of fascinating relics of the early days of the line including original locomotives and slate waggons; the second is the little maritime museum, which explains something of the remarkable story of Porthmadog as an international slate port, with the associated crafts of ship building once so important along this coast.

Borth-y-gest

Continue your walk by wandering along the edge of the harbour. Though pleasure rather than commercial craft now crowd the little port, there is still much here of interest. At the far side of the quays a dirt lane (signed as a footpath) makes its way by low cliffs and a ships' chandlers. The track eventually bears right by bollards into a lane. Keep ahead until you reach steps which descend to the right into the delightful little harbour of Borth-y-gest.

This is another little slate harbour, now largely silted up. With its great curve of quayside and cottages it still has great charm, as well as a welcoming tearoom, shop and loos.

Follow the old harbourside road at the end of which a short length of steps, right, lead into Amanda Terrace. Ignore the No Through Road sign - as the road ends a path between bollards leads onwards around the headland.

Black Rock Sands

Path finding from here is more a question of instinct than careful mapwork, but highly rewarding along a lovely stretch of coast. You begin with a beautiful, sandy path around the cove, soon going through dunes. At a broad opening in the dunes bear right onto a narrow, deep way towards white houses ahead. Steps lead up behind these onto a cobbled track. Turn left here. Beyond garages and a turning area the path continues, deep and narrow, down steps and through bracken.

This finally joins a track at a footpath sign, going right through a metal gate then immediately left, back into the bracken. There are lovely views across to the estuary. Soon you reach steps with a handrail - descend with care. Follow the path downhill (ignore the path bearing right uphill to the caravan site) making for the beach and a sycamore tree growing out of the headland. The path continues round behind a red lifebelt stand - follow the fence around the rocky headland, by the golf course. This is Ynys Cyngar: a plaque explains the association of this place with St. Cyngar.

Make your way around the headland - if the tide is out descend to the beach. The next $1^1/2$ miles are along Black Rock Sands - a wide expanse of golden beach, in the summer months shared by cars and family beach parties. You are heading for Craig Ddu - Black Rock - ahead. The only problem is about half a mile along the beach, where a fast flowing stream has to be crossed. Cross closer to the sea edge where its waters broaden and shallow over the quite firm sands.

About 200 metres from Craig Ddu, go through a gate in the fence, right, leading into the end of Black Rock Camping Park. Turn left on the track by tents or caravans parallel to the fence - as you approach what looks like an impenetrable cliff face you will see a path marked by white arrows which zigzags steeply up the hillside between brambles and bracken - a steep but perfectly safe and easy path. Ascend it, turning left into the stony lane at the top of the hill. This is a fine little viewpoint back across to the sea and mountains, but continue through the gate left, ignoring another gate to the immediate left but after a few yards bearing left along the edge of open pasture along a wallside. Keep inside the wire fence as the path now swings right over the summit of the little headland. You soon enjoy views across Criccieth Bay with the Castle directly ahead.

Criccieth

Your path descends the far side of the headland, going down the slope before picking up the path which runs along the line of an old wall. It then moves ahead to a white step stile over the railway, the site of a former rail halt serving Black Rock Sands. Cross the line, now keeping left along the railway. Path and railway soon squeeze under the shadow of Rhiw-for-fawr crag and past a shallow pond before the path dips through a tunnel under the tracks and along an enclosed way into Criccieth. Keep ahead at the level crossing gates before bearing left to the promenade and centre of this attractive little town and resort.

Give yourself time before the return train journey to explore Criccieth's splendid Castle perched on its great headland above the town's steep streets. It was founded in 1230 by Llywelyn the Great and eventually recaptured from the English by the redoubtable Owain Glyndwr. A heritage centre by the Castle relates the story of this and other castles along the coast.

Criccieth is also extremely well supplied with tea shops, restaurants and pubs. Make time before returning to the station to climb to the castle headland to see the fine views along the Lleyn peninsula to the west. The railway station is just off the A497 on the Pwllheli side of town.

Walk 6: Welshpool and Castle Caereinion

Landranger Maps: Sheets 125 and 126.

Pathfinder Maps: Sheets 887, 888 (SJ00/10. SJ20/30).

Starting Station: Welshpool (B.R.).

Finishing Station: Castle Caereinion - Welshpool & Llanfair Railway. (B.R. Timetable 75).

Distance: 5 miles (8 km) to Castle Caereinion, 12 miles (15 km) if returning to Welshpool along lanes.

Time Required: Two to three hours to Castle Caereinion railway station, four to five hours for the circular walk.

Grade: Easy to Moderate.

Possible Cut-off Point: No suitable point.

Terrain: Pastoral and wooded hill country with lengthy, but not steep, climbs in places.

Refreshment and Accommodation: The Red Lion at Castle Caereinion serves meals and there is local accommodation. Welshpool has numerous cafes and inns in addition to a good choice of overnight accommodation. The nearest youth hostel is in Shrewsbury.

Tourist Information: Vicarage Garden Car Park, Welshpool, Powys, SY21 7DD. Tel. (0938)2043/4038.

Welshpool & Llanfair Light Railway, The Station, Llanfair Caereinion, Powys, SY21 0SF. Tel (0938) 810441.

THE RAIL JOURNEY

Welshpool is first stop on the line from Shrewsbury to Aberystwyth, now known as the Cambrian Line. The journey begins in gentle Shropshire countryside but before long the impressive Breidden hills appear to the right. Welshpool's station comes as quite a surprise. It is built in a 'French Chateau' style and of such size that the startled passenger wonders why Welshpool received lavish treatment. The explanation is that the station also served as the headquarters of the then- Cambrian Railways, though only for two years. The awnings and some of the ironwork still remain and fortunately it is now a Grade II listed building. The once extensive goods yard and the area which previously accommodated the Welshpool and Llanfair Light Railway can also be seen clearly from the train.

The Welshpool & Llanfair Light Railway

One of the Great Little Trains of Wales, this 2ft 6in narrow gauge light railway has an international flavour about it, having obtained rolling stock from many different parts of the world. This diversity adds interest to an eight mile journey through rolling countryside between Welshpool and the small market town of Llanfair Caereinion.

The line was built in the early part of this century, another local project driven into existence with the hope of opening up this agricultural area. It carried both passengers and freight until the mid 1930s, when passenger traffic ceased. The line still carried goods, however, squeezing through the back streets of Welshpool to the terminus in the Cambrian Railways goods yard by Welshpool station. This ceased in the mid 1950s and the line's future remained uncertain for a number of years.

A New Lease of Life

In 1963, a group of volunteers began to restore the line and by 1981 the entire route was re-opened to passenger trains, thanks to the determination and persistence of dedicated supporters. Like the other narrow gauge steam railways in Wales this line introduces you to the scenery of Mid Wales in a very special way. It runs during an extended summer season only and it will be necessary to check return times in

Welshpool before setting off on your ramble. A return walking route (7 miles) is suggested if there is no suitable service.

If you want to travel the entire line however, you can always pick up the train at the end of your walk at Castle Caereinion and travel to Llanfair before returning to Welshpool - but remember the last train from Llanfair to Welshpool is about 1600 hours.

A welcome break on the Welshpool and Llanfair Light Railway.

THE WALK

Leave the Welshpool B.R. station building by the car park and cross the road into Severn Street. It is five minutes walk directly ahead into the town centre.

Welshpool

The route is not without interest. The Canal buildings at Welshpool

Wharf, to your left, have recently been restored and this is a good point to start any exploration of the Montgomery Canal which is year by year being rejuvenated. This truly rural navigation was first opened in 1796 and enjoyed years of prosperity before losing completely to the railways. The warehouses you see today date from the 1880s and enjoyed less than forty years activity before the canal began to decline considerably before a final abandonment in 1944. Once again, however, in its new role as a leisure facility, the canal is beginning to revive with the introduction of boat hire and narrow boat trips during the summer season.

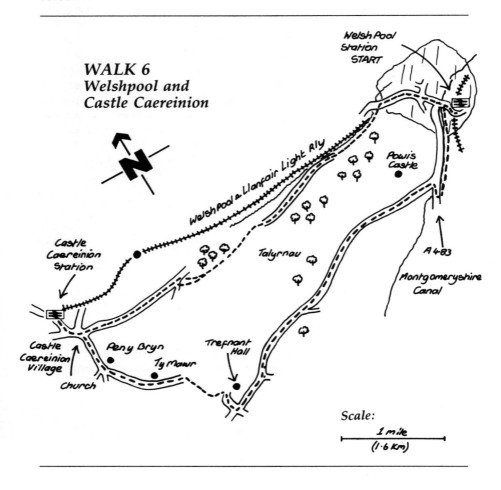

WALK 6
Welshpool and
Castle Caereinion

Welsh Pool Station START

Welsh Pool & Llanfair Light Rly

Powis Castle

Castle Caereinion Station

Talyrnau

A 483

Montgomeryshire Canal

Castle Caereinion Village

Peny Bryn

Ty Mawr

Trefnant Hall

Church

Scale:
1 mile
(1·6 Km)

The town has a number of distinctive Georgian buildings and a good selection of traditional shops, and enjoys a reasonable tourist trade. One unusual building, the brick built Cockpit, has been restored to good condition but thankfully is no longer used. Other attractions include the Powys Museum and nearby Powis Castle, a significant National Trust property.

Powis Castle

There is a footpath from the left of the High Street which leads through magnificently landscaped parkland to the castle. This fine building dates from the late thirteenth century with many sixteenth century and later improvements. The castle contains superb furniture, paintings and tapestries. It also houses relics of Clive of India, having been passed by the Herberts to the Clive family in the eighteenth century. The formal gardens and the more ruggedly landscaped park are of exceptional interest, being the work of the contentious but much loved landscape gardener, Capability Brown. By combining a trip on the Welshpool and Llanfair Light Railway, a visit to Powis Castle and some country walking, a few days in Welshpool offers a stimulating break.

Powis Castle

Outskirts of Welshpool

From the Canal continue ahead up Severn Street to the main cross roads. Cross over and again continue up Welshpool's wide thoroughfare, known at this point as High Street, but becoming Mount Street and then Raven Street. It is one long street full of traditional shops and pubs. However, if you wish to call in to the Tourist Information Centre then turn right at the main crossroads and just beyond the Spar supermarket, by the car park, is the recently built Tourist Information Centre.

Raven Street descends to Raven Square where there's a roundabout with the Welshpool and Llanfair railway terminus beyond (you might wish to check your travel times here). If not proceed as follows. As the road bears to the right by the bridge turn left along a track. The footpath is signed here and this first section is obviously well used.

This soon leads to a stile. Cross it and continue ahead to another stile; then maintain your direction ahead, continuing near to the stream. On the left the landscaped parkland of Powis Castle becomes more dominant. Continue and cross the next slanting stile by the stream where the path rises slightly to another stile. Continue ahead but move gradually up the slope and away from the stream, towards the track and the barred gate. Go through this and continue ahead along the tarmac road, passing on your right a number of interesting buildings, reflecting a style of architecture characteristic of the upper Severn valley. Avoid, however, any turnings to the right at this stage.

Eventually this path becomes rougher and leads up to a farm called Talyrnau. The track leads around to the right hand side of the buildings and then to the rear of the farmyard to a barred gate by a barn. Go through this but do not follow the more pronounced track up the field. Instead, bear slightly right towards the woodland. The path is no longer clear through this section of wood, as indicated on the map, but you have to go through the gate and bear right along the field edge until you see a track sloping down to the right alongside the wood's edge. Follow this track, go through a gate by a cascading stream and continue ahead over a brow to an isolated barn.

Walk around the barn to a track leading down to another stream and just before the stream turn left. This path leads up to and through a gateway into a field. Your way is directly across to another gate and it is here that the path becomes less distinct. You will see to your right a house, Pen-yr-wrte, and the path is shown on the map as heading diagonally across the field towards the wood. However, it is difficult to cross the field boundary at this point so use the nearest access point into the next field such as the gateway nearer to the centre of the field. Go through this and head towards the right corner of the field where there is access to the next field through a gateway. Bear right uphill to the top right corner of the field where there is an open gateway leading onto a farm access track. Bear right here and at the T junction turn left along a very quiet tarmac lane to Castle Caereinion.

Castle Caereinion

Follow this lane to Castle Caereinion. There is a beautiful view of this isolated valley to your left. The lane meets the main B4385 road at a junction. Across the road is the church and also the Red Lion public house. Turn right for the W.&L.L.R.'s Castle Caereinion Station, which is a short distance along the B4385 road. Here you can catch the train back to Welshpool - or forward to Llanfair.

The Circular Walk

If you intend to walk back to Welshpool (7 miles), the route is pleasant enough but it should be said that there is a fair amount of road walking involved. Turn left along the B4385 passing by an old chapel dating from the 1840s, now converted into a house. At the first major farm on your left called Pen-y-Bryn, go left along a tarmac lane. Follow this for some time. You then come to the ancient barn of Ty Mawr. Bear left by the barn and then the lane curves right, climbing steeply up to Upper Trefnant Hill. This track becomes a green lane, and you must avoid turn offs to the left or right. This eventually leads you to Trefnant Hall farm. The map shows a turning to the right down the slope beneath you but this is missing, so walk virtually to the farm but turn sharp right beforehand, that is, walking a V shape. This lane leads downhill to a tarmac road. Turn left here and follow this pleasant road for over two miles to the entrance of Powis Castle.

The section from the castle downwards is a little busier with traffic for the castle, so be more wary. At the main road turn right and follow the verge for a short distance to the canal. Cross the road and follow the canalside towpath the remaining mile to Severn Road where you turn right for the final five minutes' walk to Welshpool station.

Walk 7: In the Steps of the Drovers - Barmouth to Dyffryn.

Landranger Map: 124.

Outdoor Leisure Map: Sheet 18 Snowdonia (Harlech & Bala).

Starting Station: Barmouth.

Finishing Station: Dyffryn Ardudwy (B.R. Table 76).

Distance: 12 miles (20 km).

Time Required: 6 - 7 hours.

Grade: Moderate - but some strenuous sections.

Possible Cut-off Point: No real turn off point beyond Panorama Walk (2 miles).

Terrain: Moorland tracks and hillpaths.

Refreshment and Accommodation: Barmouth, then nothing until the end of the walk at Dyffryn.

Tourist Information: Station Road, Barmouth, Gwynedd, LL42 1NL. Tel: (0341) 280787

THE RAIL JOURNEY

Abermaw - Barmouth

Barmouth is a key station on the Cambrian Coast Line (see Walk Five) where trains often wait in the passing loop before continuing their journey. The little resort is an excellent centre for anyone planning a few days riding and walking from Welsh railways. There's also a very good accommodation base, ranging from comfortable medium sized hotels to modest bed and breakfast accommodation. Barmouth also has a fine sandy beach, a promenade, a choice of restaurants, cafes and ancient hostelries together with all the usual amenities of a small seaside town.

Abermaw, to give the town its Welsh name, was in pre- holiday resort days a fishing port and boatyard. It still has a small fishing harbour, though leisure craft inevitably outnumber fishing boats at the wharfs. By the harbour you'll find a white house, now a restaurant known as Ty Gwyn yn Y Bermo (The White House in Barmouth). According to tradition it was built for Gruffudd Fychan, a local nobleman, between 1460 and 1485, and may have been used by Henry Tudor, later King of England and Wales, when he plotted the downfall of Richard III.

Not far away, just in from the Harbour is another fascinating building, Ty Crwn, a circular "lock-up" or prison for offenders now used as a small heritage interpretation centre.

Catch The Ferry

If you've time in Barmouth, it's worth catching the ferry to the terminus of the Fairbourne Railway directly across from the Harbour, where the little $12^1/_2$ inch gauge steam trains operate to Fairbourne for the "Butterfly Safari". A combined ticket for boat and train can be bought in the Harbour, and you can return to Barmouth by train from Fairbourne Station.

THE WALK

From the station, turn left into Station Road, which crosses the railway at a level crossing, going right into High Street. Opposite the market place and at the side of the Cors y Gedd Hotel a National Trust sign indicates the way to Dinas Oleu up a steep street. Go straight ahead past the cross roads, following the narrow road right as directed by the National Trust sign, but keeping left at the next junction following the footpath sign. The path climbs steeply up - keep ahead by houses built on the rockside. There is a fine view across the rooftops of Barmouth. At the next National Trust sign follow the path around the headland until you reach a National Trust Cairn.

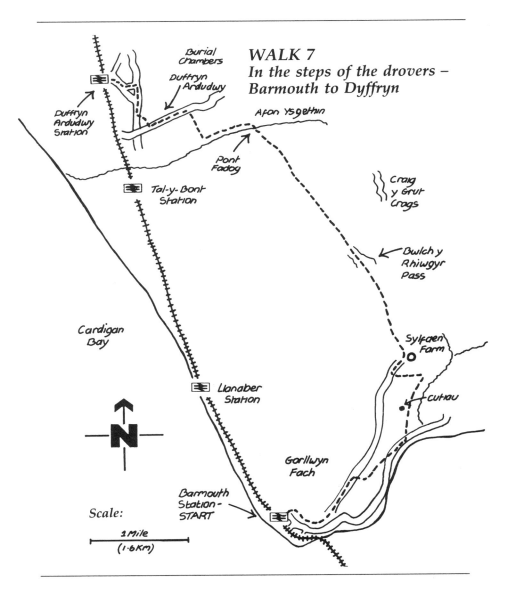

WALK 7
In the steps of the drovers –
Barmouth to Dyffryn

Burial Chambers

Duffryn Ardudwy

Duffryn Ardudwy Station

Afon Ysgethin

Pont Fadog

Tal-y-Bont Station

Craig y Grut Crags

Bwlch y Rhiwgyr Pass

Cardigan Bay

Sylfaen Farm

Cutiau

Llanaber Station

Gorllwyn Fach

N

Barmouth Station - START

Scale:

1 Mile
(1·6Km)

Dinas Oleu

Dinas Oleu - the name means "Fortress of Light" - is a $4^1/_2$ acre estate which has a niche in history as the first property acquired by the National Trust, having been given to the Trust by Mrs F. Talbot in 1895. More recently, in 1980, the Trust was able to add a further 12 acres to this superb natural viewpoint.

Your uphill path zigzags (or walk alongside the wall) to a pedestrian gate above you. The path now follows the wall to the crest of the hill giving extensive views across the estuary to Fairbourne.

The Mawddach Estuary

Panorama Walk

Keep on the broader path at the junction of ways, alongside a stone wall and through a pedestrian gate onto a track. Keep ahead through a gate onto an enclosed way which leads past a cottage, following a sign for Panorama Walk down the track into a lane. Keep left, past a narrow field and the farmhouse Hafod-y-Bryn on the right, a hundred metres past which a metal sign at a gate "To Panorama Walk" indicates a track right towards woodland. Go through a gate into the wood and after a further 100 metres down a shady track turn right through a gate onto a path which leads to the summit of a rocky headland where there is a bench. This is Panorama Walk - a quite enchanting view of the whole of the Mawddach estuary and river, looking towards the mountains of Snowdonia with Cadair Idris on the right.

Return to the gate and shady track, this time continuing downhill through delightful woodland. At a junction of tracks, all signed, your way is left. At a tarmac track turn left, uphill.

Cutliau

You eventually reach Cutliau where there is a tiny chapel (now a private house) with a scatter of gravestones. Your way is through the metal gate below the chapel, a stony path between walls. Soon after passing power lines you reach a junction of green ways. The footpath is to the right, swinging across a little stream and through a broad metal gate into woodland. Keep directly ahead now up through the wood, through another gate and across another little stream. At a fork keep ahead on the main path which finally emerges into the open with superb views across the Mawddach valley to the right. As you return to the woodland you reach a junction. Your way is now sharp left up a bridleway which climbs back through the wood to a gate. Do not go through here - stay in the wood zigzagging uphill by the wall to the top of the wood where you follow the wall to a gate by a barn. Go through here to a lane which you follow right uphill towards Sylfaen Farm.

Cerrig Arthur

Just before Sylfaen Farm look for a stony track left leading to a gate where you take the left of twin tracks climbing alongside the wall. As you climb you enjoy ever more splendid views of Cadair Idris's massive bulk to the right. Keep along the wall through the field, soon passing Cerrig Arthur, the remnants of a Bronze Age stone circle in an impressive setting. Keep on the track into the next field past a spring, but look for a gate on the left about 80 metres beyond the spring through which the right-of-way goes, leaving the track. Your way is to the right to the gate in the middle of the next field wall (keep to the left to avoid marshy ground) then into the next field climbing left to another gate. From here you'll find a grassy path climbing the moor - a steep ascent - to a gate at the summit.

Bwlch y Rhiwgr

From this point the route joins and follows an ancient drovers road from Dolgellau to Harlech through Bwlch y Rhiwgr which is a deep, narrow pass, some 420 metres (1,300 feet) above sea level. As you cross the pass at a stile, the landscape and seascape unfolds to the north - a huge panorama across the northern part of Cardigan Bay with the Lleyn Peninsula and its hills etched along the horizon.

Llety Lloegr

There is much easier walking now, along an old, rocky path deep sunken in places from the passage of many thousands of hooves, through a wild, desolate landsacpe. This is an ancient public highway (therefore not shown as a green footpath on O.S. maps). But walking and pathfinding are much easier now. Keep ahead to a gate and footbridge, looking out for a line of white posts designed to help the walker. The path follows past the first field, then cuts across the next open field to rejoin wall and fence passing the grassy outlines of another prehistoric circle. Maintain the same direction due northwest, the path finally emerging at Pont Fadog, an old drovers' bridge over the Afon Ysgethin. A few metres further along the track, now a tarmac road, is Llety Lloegr, the lodging house for the English (the 18th century drovers who took their herds of black Welsh cattle through Bwlch y Rhiwgr Pass to the Midlands were mainly English). Llety Lloegr now serves very welcome tea and scones to - mainly English - ramblers.

If you've time, it's worth walking another 200 metres along the lane where, on the left, you'll find the great stone slabs of a prehistoric burial chamber.

Woodlands

Otherwise, return to Pont Fadog, at the side of which you'll find a footpath, signed, which leads along a delightful riverside path down the Ysgethin, through deciduous woods.

As the path finally swings away from the river about half a mile below Pont Fadog it reaches a junction of ways. Keep to the right hand, higher path which joins a broader track. Keep right here through oak and birch trees. As the end of the wood approaches you come to another junction. Keep right along the edge of the wood, following the fence, across a stile to a gate. Head towards the gate ahead near power lines and a step stile by a house.

Dyffryn Burial Chamber

Turn left here, following the lane downhill for about 400 metres to where, opposite a farmtrack, you'll find a footpath sign at a gate, on the right. The path crosses to a wall, and on the right to a stile. It continues below the wood to a second stile by a stream through woodland, then bears diagonally left across an open field. Immediately to your left, in a little enclosed area, is Dyffryn Burial Chamber, a site developed by Neolithic farmers some 3,500 years before Christ. Later generations added a cairn and second burial chamber.

The path from the burial chamber leads to the long main street of Dyffryn Ardudwy, or you can retrace your steps and take a back path through the village to avoid road walking. You'll find shops and cafes in the village, but allow a good ten minutes' walk to the station. Turn left at the post office,following the lane to the right, and left at the junction to the station by its level crossing. The Cadwgan Hotel nearby might well provide you with refreshment and alternative waiting accommodation to the little shelter on the station platform.

Walk 8: Talyllyn

Landranger Map: Sheet 124.

Outdoor Leisure Map: Sheet 23 Snowdonia (Cadair Idris).

Starting Station: Nant Gwernol (Talyllyn Railway).

Finishing Station: Morfa Mawddach (B.R. table 76).

Distance: 8 miles (13km).

Time required: 5 hours.

Grade: Moderate - but with one strenuous section.

Possible Cut-off Point: Bodilan Fach - return to Abergynolwyn for Talyllyn train or Gwynedd Bus 30.

Terrain: Hill tracks, paths and lanes. One very steep ascent of over 400 metres (1,200 feet) from Bodilan Fach to Trawsfynydd.

Refreshment and Accommodation: Cafeteria on Talyllyn Railway at Tywyn, pub and cafe in Abergynolwyn village. Ample accommodation in Tywyn and Barmouth (reached by train or $1^1/_2$ mile walk over the viaduct from Morfa). Youth hostel at Kings - four miles from the end of the walk.

Tourist Information: High Street, Tywyn, Gwynedd, LL36 9AD Tel. (0654) 710070; Station Road, Barmouth, Gwynedd LL42 1NL. Tel.(0341) 280787.

The Talyllyn Railway, Wharf Station, Tywyn, Gwynedd, LL36 9EY Tel (0654) 710472

THE RAIL JOURNEY

The Talyllyn Railway is reached by an easy two minute walk from Tywyn Station on the Cambrian Coast Line, simply turn right out of the station.

This 2 foot 3 inch gauge line was opened in 1865 to bring slate from an isolated valley at Bryn Eglwys above Abergynolwyn to the Cambrian Railways from where it was transhipped onto standard gauge waggons at Tywyn. The line carried regular passenger services as far as Abergynolwyn right up to the 1950s when, facing closure, it was taken over by the Talyllyn Railway Preservation Society to become the first preserved steam railway in the world.

The Society, with a dedicated team of volunteers and a high degree of professionalism, has run the railway ever since. The passenger line was actually extended as far as Nant Gwernol in 1976 along what had hitherto been a minerals-only tramway, a scenically splendid section of line without road access.

The Railway is also noteworthy for having some of the oldest original locomotives in the world still working its tracks, most notably "Talyllyn" dating from 1864 and "Dolgoch" from 1866. Even when inevitable repairs and rebuilds are taken into account, these are essentially the same engines that have been steaming up the valley for more than 120 years.

A Classic Journey

The rail journey from Tywyn is a classic narrow gauge trip. It moves from the valley floor in the little coastal town and resort of Tywyn to begin a steady and continuous climb, gradually gaining height on the hillside through Rhydyronen and Brynglas, and finally reaching the superb wooded gorge containing Dolgoch Falls, only a short walk away from Dolgoch Station. Beyond Dolgoch the scenery becomes ever more impressive. Abergynolwyn station is finally reached about half a mile above the village, positioned there because of easier road access. The final ascent, on the ledge of the hillside to Nant Gwernol above the thickly forested gorge, provides a starting point for some beautiful forest walks.

Abergynolwyn Station on the Talyllyn Railway

THE WALK

Leave Nant Gwernol station along the platform exit, following the Forest Trails. Bear left at the fork to cross the footbridge across the Nant Gwernol gorge, bearing left downhill down a richly wooded ravine. You are quite likely to see the little train start its return journey, having run round its carriages, chuffing along the rocky ledge above you, between the trees.

Abergynolwyn

The path crosses a stile and little knoll, and then joins a farmtrack. Keep left downhill into Abergynolwyn. This former quarry village was once linked to its railway by a rope incline, parts of which survive together with other relics of the slate industry. You'll pass a welcoming coffee shop on the left and, as you turn left on the main B4405 through the edge of the village, the Railway Inn on your right, which serves pub food and real ale.

Afon Dysynni

Continue to the road bridge over the stream, immediately prior to which a track, right, leads off. Follow this to a footbridge. Cross here, and take the paved way towards the cottage ahead, but follow the path as it bears right below the cottage garden. You will soon cross a little slab bridge and a stile. The path now follows the valley some 50 metres above the stream - a lovely clear way contouring around the narrow valley of the Afon Dysynni. This river flows from Lake Talyllyn, a glacial lake some 3 miles away at the head of the pass, and this narrow valley through the hills has clearly been carved out by glacial meltwaters.

The path is easy to follow, crossing the occasional stile, and going round (waymarked) a slight landslip. It emerges at a gate to the immediate right of Rhiwlas Farm by a bridge called Pont Ystumanner. Cross, but leave the lane at a gate on the left, just past the bridge. Here the public right of way follows the river for a further 200 metres, where, as the river begins to bear left, the path follows the line of an old hedge to a gate on the right into the lane. Turn left along the lane.

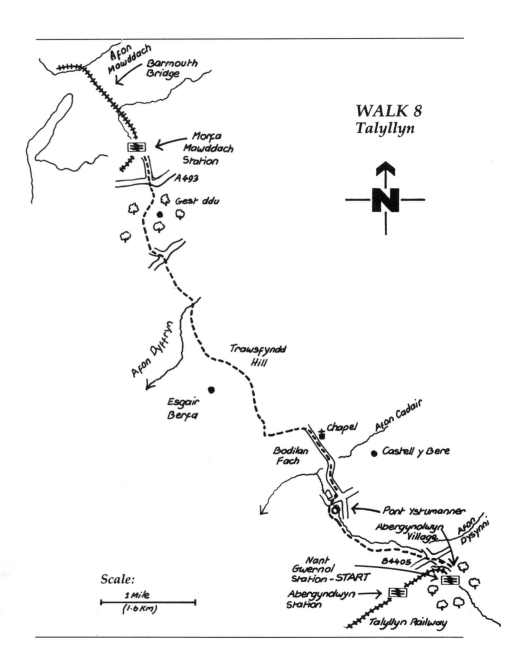

Afon
Mawddach

Barmouth
Bridge

WALK 8
Talyllyn

N

Morfa
Mawddach
Station

A493

Gest ddu

Afon Dyffryn

Trawsfyndd
Hill

Esgair
Berfa

Afon Cadair

Chapel

Castell y Bere

Bodilan
Fach

Pont Ystrumanner

Abergynolwyn
Village

Afon
Dysynni

Nant
Gwernol
Station - START

B4405

Abergynolwyn
Station

Scale:

1 Mile
(1.6 Km)

Talyllyn Railway

Castell-y-bere

From here there is a fine view across to a remote and strange hilltop castle on a isolated crag about half a mile to your right. This is Castell-y-Bere, built by Prince Llywelyn the Great around 1221 but captured by Edward in 1283 and abandoned in 1295. There is access to the ruins and it can be reached by lane and fieldpath.

Continue along the lane in the same direction for nearly a mile, crossing the river by a bridge, to the hamlet of Bodilan Fach where you'll find a tiny chapel and a pillar box emptied just twice a week.

The climb

Go through the gate into the farm at Bodilan. Continue past the farm, keeping ahead along the track up the valley, but about 100 metres beyond the farm, go through a gate, signposted, which leads to a narrow grassy track, left, climbing steeply up the hillside.

This is the start of an extremely long ascent, so take your time and enjoy the views as you go. The green track climbs between walls and through gates and seems to be joining a far better used stony track heading towards the wood ahead. But it doesn't - keep sharp right on the grassy way alongside the hedge and fence, steeply uphill to a gate above the wood. Keep ahead now in the same direction, steeply up the breast of the hill.

As you ascend, the views across the surrounding hills are increasingly impressive. One fascinating geological feature in the valley below you is the fact that until relatively recent times this was part of a deep river estuary of the Dysynni River. This is now silted up, drained and reclaimed as farmland, but the line of hills ahead were once sea crags, most notably the pointed Craig yr Aderyn - the Birds' Rock - which continued to be occupied by a colony of cormorants long after the sea had departed.

You are soon crossing open moorland along the track which eventually runs alongside a wire fence. The climb continues as the track bears sharp right along the fence, climbing up to gateway beyond which a stony track is reached. Keep ahead. The gradient, to the relief of aching legs and lungs, finally begins to ease but about 100 metres after the next gateway do not be lured into following the stone track as it curves left - your path is along a fainter green way which bears right, about 50 metres above the drystone wall, to a gate ahead. You should be heading almost due north, above the steep sides of a deep mountain corrie. Go through a gate ahead. The path eventually merges with a stone track which swings above the head of a quarry. Look for a ladder stile (signposted) in the fence on the left which leads to a path which contours around the summit of Trawsfynydd. Esgair Berfa is the peak to your left and a shallow valley, through which runs a farm road, lies below you. Keep curving round, finally losing a little height as you approach the track.

Bronze Age remains

The path finally joins the farm track at the summit of a narrow pass. Turn right here for two hundred metres, crossing a stream. Look for a stile on the left by a red fire post - this leads to a narrow path over the brow of the hill by a large Cairn, almost certainly a Bronze Age tumulus. The path now begins to descend steeply through the forest and as it does so there are quite breathtaking views across and up the Mawddach estuary and the hills above Barmouth.

Oak and birch woods

You reach a tarmac road. Cross to a stile and follow the track to Cyfanned Fawr farm. The track, a lovely walled green lane, passes the farm and swings to the right, where it descends steeply towards woodland. Keep right as a track joins from the left, but as the track swings sharp left down into a wood of oak and pale birch trees, look for a narrow linking path (the right of way) about 20 metres from the bend which links with a track below to the right. Follow this next track through a disused quarry. Keep ahead to where it seems to enter a field, where waymarks will direct you right over a stile and down a narrow, sunken track. Keep ahead here to where a kissing gate at a signpost leads you to the right, downhill, bearing slightly left to a ladder stile at a quarry road. Cross to the continuation of the path down to the main Dolgellau road and to a stile alongside a row of terraced houses and their gardens.

Morfa Mawddach

Turn left in the lane where almost immediately you'll see the BR sign on the station drive for Morfa Mawddach. Where this lane opens to a cross roads, a stile on the left takes you along the last few metres of the old Barmouth-Dolgellau-Wrexham railway line, closed in 1965 and now the Morfa Mawddach Walk along the estuary to Dolgellau. The old station platforms survive - the site of public toilets and a small car park where local people leave their cars to walk into Barmouth.

Trains at Morfa Mawddach's surviving working platform will take you either into Barmouth or back towards Tywyn. If you've more than half an hour to wait, you might consider it worth walking just a little over a mile across the famous Barmouth Bridge. This is a pedestrian toll bridge shared with the railway. It has some excellent views and, in Barmouth, there is a choice of cafes and pubs which you might sample before catching your train at Barmouth Station.

Walk 9: Along Glyndwr's Way

Landranger Map: Sheet 148.

Pathfinder Map: Sheet 950 (SO 27/37).

Starting Station: Llangynllo.

Finishing Station: Knighton (B.R. Table 129).

Distance: 7 to 8 miles (12 km approx).

Time Required: 4 hours.

Grade: Moderate.

Possible Cut-off Point: At Fountain Head, about 4 miles (6 km), a tarmac lane leads to Heyop and Knucklas.

Terrain: The walk is mainly along rough tracks with a lesser amount of road walking. There are some climbs but they are not steeply graded.

Refreshment and Accommodation: Knighton offers a plentiful supply of both including a Youth Hostel.

Tourist Information: Offa's Dyke Heritage Centre, The Old School, Knighton offers local information. Tel. (0547) 528753 or Rock Park Spa, Llandrindod Wells, Powys, LD1 6AA. Tel. (0597) 2600.

THE RAIL JOURNEY

The Heart of Wales Line, known also as the Central Wales Line, must surely be one of the remotest in Wales and is held in great affection by local traveller and visitor alike. The Victorian railway builders, ever optimistic about their plans, had real desires for this to become a major artery between the North West, Swansea and North America. In reality local interests developed different sections from the late 1850s and these smaller companies were absorbed by the powerful London and North Western Railway, while the Great Western Railway showed continuing interest at the southern end.

Fight for Existence

In its heyday the route served the purpose of a trunk route carrying both freight and passenger traffic between the North of England and South West Wales as well as serving the rural communities along the line. If long distance traffic has declined, the line is still extremely important because it serves many villages and townships in this otherwise isolated part of rural Mid Wales. The struggle of local people to keep their line open in spite of what has in the past been the indifference of central government led to the formation of the Heart of Wales Line Travellers Association. The Association is specifically interested in making sure that the line continues into the twenty-first century and in promoting the line for tourism. Among excellent recent initiatives has been the "Recreational Rambler" Sunday shuttle service supported by Dyfed and Powys County Councils and the Sports Council for Wales, linked to an imaginative programme of walks and countryside activities. Enquire at local tourist offices for information about future activities on the line.

You can be assured of a scenically inspiring ride along the 90 mile stretch of this single line railway between Craven Arms and Llanelli. Not only are there views along tranquil valleys but also of the Cambrian Mountains and Brecon Beacons, of hamlets and spas, of rivers flowing pure in their infancy. There are glimpses of rural Welsh life, of villagers travelling to the market towns of Llandeilo, Llanymddyfri (Llandovery) or Knighton as well as the elegant old spa and inland resort of Llandrindod Wells - an excellent centre from which to explore the delights of the Heart of Wales Line.

Knighton and Offa's Dyke

The Welsh name for Knighton is Tref y Clawdd. This means 'The town on the Dyke' and in this respect it is unusual in that it is the only town situated on the line of Offa's Dyke throughout its entire length. The ancient defensive boundary, dating from the 8th century, was thought to have been at least 30 feet high with a 15 foot ditch alongside. Offa, King of Mercia was obviously very determined to keep the warlike Welshmen at bay. Similarly, particularily during the years of the Marcher Lords, Welshmen were anxious to keep Englishmen out. The consequence for Tref y Clawdd has been centuries of considerable strife and bloodshed, happily now confined to the memory of history.

Offa's Dyke is now one of Britain's most popular Long Distance Footpath Routes, and Knighton is a mid way point on the 168 mile route and on one of its most attractive sections.

The Battle of Pilleth

It wasn't just along Offa's Dyke where Welsh and English swords clashed. About two miles south west of Knighton, at Bryn Glas Pilleth, Owain Glyndwr inflicted a crushing defeat on the army of Herefordshire nobleman Edmund Mortimer at the Battle of Pilleth in June 1402, when well over a thousand Marcher troops were slaughtered and then brutally mutilated. The trees planted at Bryn Glas mark the spot where the bones of some of the dead were subsequently found. Sir Edmund was captured but later became an ally of Glyndwr, marrying his daughter before eventually dying in the siege of Harlech.

Needless to say the Welsh Marches are much quieter now. Situated on the shoulders of the Teme valley between the uplands of the Frydd and Panpunton, Knighton is an agricultural town with many narrow streets and a number of Tudor houses. It has not been modernised extensively and this adds considerably to its overall character. Thursday is market day but it is mainly livestock which is sold. The town really is a lovely centre for walking.

THE WALK

Owain Glyndwr's Way

Owain Glyndwr's Way was created by Powys County Council as a "themed" long distance route. It uses existing rights of way mainly and visits many of the places specifically associated with the romantic figure of Owain Glyndwr, perhaps Wales' greatest national hero, including, at Machynlleth, the location of his Parliament and the countryside in which he roamed with his guerilla armies. The route is 130 miles long between Knighton and Welshpool and can be done as a circular route with the addition of a further 20 miles along the Offa's Dyke Path.

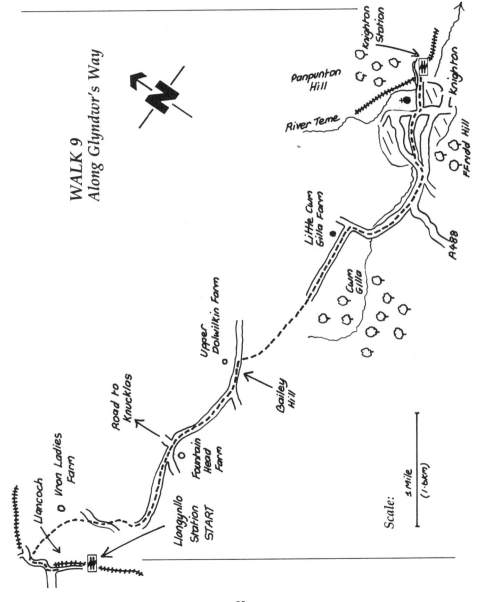

WALK 9
Along Glyndwr's Way

You can find full details of the walk in a series of leaflets available from Powys County Council (County Hall, Llandrindod Wells, Powys) or in Richard Sale's quite excellent, detailed historical guide *Owain Glyndwr's Way* (Hutchinson).

This short section of the route between Llangynllo and Knighton is an appetiser for the full Owain Glyndwr's Way. You are bound to return for more!

A Haunted Tunnel

Come out of Llangynllo station, by a house which once belonged to the railway company, and then turn right. After the bustle of the train the quietness will come as something of a shock but you will soon become attuned to this wild upland territory. Continue along this lane passing Llangoch farm. Underneath is Llangynllo Tunnel, said to be haunted by a legendary engine driver from Knighton. You'll soon see where Glyndwr's Way leads off to the left in the direction of Abbey Cwm Hir but this is not the direction to be taken on this occasion. The tarmac lane begins to climb and soon a barred gate appears on the right, signed Glyndwr's Way. Go through it and continue upwards along a track keeping the hedge to your left. This leads up to a gateway which opens out onto moorland; again keep the hedge to your left. The track begins to drop, with views of the Heyop valley to the left, to a junction of tracks with a small Welsh farm on the left. The way is directly ahead through a barred gate and continues ahead beyond the old quarry. Go through another two barred gates until you reach a tarmac lane.

Turn right onto the lane and as this begins to descend there is a barred gate on your left, again waymarked. The track climbs up and winds around to the right and up to another barred gate where there are good views of the railway station where you started an hour ago. As you can see, this is isolated country where the farming community has to struggle against the elements to make a living. To your right, in this farming panorama you can just pick out Llangynllo village, some distance from the railway station.

Cut-off Point to Knucklas

You meet a tarmac road coming up from Fron-goch. Continue ahead to Fountain Head where there is a turning to the left. This is your cut-off point to Knucklas by way of Heyop, a hamlet where you turn right. Knucklas is a pleasant village nestled beneath the ruins of Cnwclas Castle. Some of the material used to build the impressive thirteen arch railway viaduct no doubt came from the decaying fortress. Possibly that's why the builders felt it necessary to add the ornate battlements at each end. Make sure that there is a suitable train before you set off to Knucklas.

Bailey Hill

If you are completing the walk to Knighton then make your way along the lane and continue straight ahead at the junction mentioned above. This leads to Bailey Hill and from here onwards it is downhill for most of the walk. The road curves to the right and on your left is Upper Dolwilkin farm. Beyond is Knucklas. Not far along now is your turning to the right which is waymarked. It is refreshing to return to tracks and paths and this final section is fine walking. At the first meeting of tracks bear left. Walk down the field with the hedge now on your right. Go over the stream, with Downes's Dingle to your right falling away to Cwm Gilla, and proceed through the gateway.

Continue uphill with the hawthorn hedge to your left and up to another gate. Your way becomes a muddy lane descending the shoulder of Cwm Gilla . This in turn becomes a tarmac lane and curves round to the right with a stream hurtling down alongside it. Follow this lane down beyond the bungalows to a bridge by Brookhouse Farm. Turn left at the main A488 road.

By the petrol station turn left and then right along a delightful access way to Knighton town centre. The sight of dwellings must have been a welcome sight for many a weary traveller coming down from the hills in unsettled times. The town's inns and cafes are still a comfort to the tired walker.

Walk 10: Llandrindod Wells

Landranger Map: Sheet 147.

Pathfinder Map: Sheet 970 (SO06/16).

Starting Station: Penybont.

Finishing Station: Llandrindod Wells (B.R. Table 129).

Distance: 7 miles (11 km).

Time Required: 4 hours.

Grade: Moderate.

Possible Cut-off Point: No suitable point.

Terrain: Gentle countryside along recently signed paths but with some steep climbs and rough paths in places.

Refreshment and Accommodation: Plentiful supply of hotels, guest houses, good pubs and cafes in Llandrindod Wells. Nearest Youth Hostel is at Knighton on the Heart of Wales Line.

Tourist Information: Rock Park Spa, Llandrindod Wells, Powys, LD1 6AA. Tel. (0597) 2600.

THE RAIL JOURNEY

Llandrindod Wells is by far the busiest intermediate station on the scenic Heart of Wales line and is one of the very few to be staffed. With restricted access to longer distance bus or coach services, the town depends very heavily on the railway as a lifeline. The arrival of the train is something of an occasion; people are picked up by some local hotels and farmhouses; locals come to meet friends and go shopping.

Llandrindod Wells

This Victorian Spa is very charming. It is a quiet town full of hotels and guest houses built to serve the growing trade of the last century. The sick and infirm came for medicinal purposes and to drink the mineral waters, the rich to see and be seen. All enjoyed days of contentment in this little Spa town with its setting of lush green hills.

The air still has a freshness about it and you will find no difficulty in finding a place to have a coffee while reading the morning papers. The Rock Spa Pump Room, where you'll also find the Tourist Information Office, still offers waters to taste, not one but three different kinds and served on handpump. Why not take a glass of natural Magnesium, Saline or Sulphur water, but perhaps at the end of your walk for at least one of the sparkling waters is reputed to have a purgative effect! If you are an admirer of Victorian costume make sure that you time your visit to coincide with the Llandindod Victorian Festival which takes place in early September each year.

Llandrindod is an ideal base for several of the walks in this book. Not only can you use the railway to visit Knighton, Llanwrtyd Wells and the like but there are also local buses to Builth, Rhayader and the Elan valley. The Post Buses are a particularily fascinating piece of local rural transport and visit hamlets and quiet backwaters that coaches do not penetrate. Enquire at the Post Office for details and timetables.

THE WALK

Take the train to Penybont. This is a request stop, as are many of the unmanned stations along this line, which means you must inform the guard of your intention to alight before you board the train.

At Penybont station leave by the main station approach and at the main A44 road turn left and cross over to walk facing the traffic along a short section of road. Pass by a milestone and as the road curves right and then left, opposite a small group of trees in a hollow, turn right through a gateway. Walk ahead, keeping the fence to the right. You come to a gateway on the left. Go through it and turn right, and for a few metres walk along the edge before turning slightly right across the field towards the house. Cross the stile onto the tarmac lane and bear right. Follow this lane for approximately a mile (2 km) until you reach the main A483 road. As the lane begins to descend there's a fine view of Crossgates Church and Church House farm.

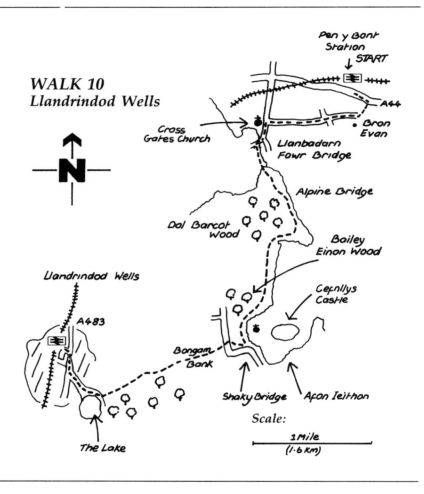

Go left along a short distance of the main road across the bridge and although it looks as if there is no way down you will notice a small gap in the crash barrier on the left and a narrow path leading down the embankment into the flood meadow. Head for the wood a field's distance away where the indistinct path rises up to a stile. The path becomes less clear as you make your way ahead at first. Turn back down and slightly left on the track to the gateway. Your way ahead is diagonally across the field to the far right hand corner. Go over the stile next to the gate and follow the field boundary to the corner and then left. This becomes more of a track and it can become very wet at certain times of the year on this section. Keep ahead to the barred gate where you will see the ford on the left and a farm to the right.

Alpine Bridge

Proceed uphill passing the bridge over the Afon Ieithon, known locally as the Alpine Bridge. This leads up to the remains of an old castle thought to date from the early twelfth century. The bridge was said to have originally been a large fallen tree but the present structure looks a little more secure.

Once beyond the bridge your way is to the left, rather than on the main track, through a gate and along a path which is signposted. Walk slightly right downwards to the stream which you cross, then continue ahead through the wood to a gate. Go through it and after a short distance bear right, between two parallel thorn hedgerows as indicated by the finger post. Keep closer to the thorns on your right and behind a great oak there is another finger post directing you right, up the track to a stile where you enter the wood. This next section is a delightful stretch of path, with broad leaved woodland, rich in wildlife, around you, and the pure waters of the Afon Ieithon below. The path is, however, narrow in places and requires some care in negotiation at times. It eventually falls, almost literally, to a tributary stream, guarded by two stiles, and then enters rough pasture. Go straight ahead to a stile to the right of the white boundary marker. Cross the track and opposite, slightly to your right is a stile leading into the next field. Go over it and keep as close as is feasible to the fence on your left.

The Short Cut Bridge

Go over the next stile, with Glanyrafon to your left, and continue ahead keeping company with the hedge on your left to the corner. Near to here it is said that there was once a fragile bridge provided for the then curate to hurry across to St Michael's Church in time for the service.

Bailey Einon Wood

Bear left here and this leads to a stile in a marshy area. Continue ahead, now with hedge to your right to Bailey Einon wood. Fortunately, this land is now in the care of the Hereford and Radnorshire Trust and the path ahead is open to Shaky Bridge. The wood is still coppiced and is thus very much more attractive to wildlife than the monotonous coniferous plantations which cover some parts of Mid Wales. Proceed through the wood to Shaky Bridge.

Cefnllys Castle

Over the other side of the bridge is St Michael's Church. In the 1890s the local curate, perhaps the one who used the footbridge, in a desperate bid to persuade his dwindling parishioners to worship in Llandrindod Wells, had the roof removed. Needless to say the indignant parishioners had it reinstated five years later having saved up the necessary money. The earthworks above probably date back to an early Welsh camp of some description but the natural defensive site was used in the 13th century by Ralph Mortimer to build a castle. It was ransacked by Llywelyn ap Gruffydd, Prince of Wales, but returned to the Marcher Lords who exacted considerable revenge on the local population for the deed.

Before the tarmac road leading to Shaky Bridge, however, there is a stile on the right. Cross it and head slightly right uphill. This becomes steeper before it reaches a stile leading onto the tarmac road. Cross the lane and go through the barred gate opposite. While not shown on Ordnance Survey maps, this path is waymarked ahead. Keep the hedge to your right. There are several marvellous views from here across to Cefnllys Castle.

Keep ahead and cross the next stile where you will see the remains of an old delivery van. Go left and follow the track now curving around the hillside to the right. Do not continue on this track but bear off, slightly left, towards the field corner to the left of the hilltop.

By the lake

Continue ahead to a stile leading into a recent plantation. Cross the stile and walk along the fence on your left until you come to another stile. Do not cross it but bear right along a clear path through the trees to another stile. You can now see Llandrindod Wells ahead. Continue downhill to the far left hand corner of the field and there you will find a small gateway leading into the woodland. Walk through this superb woodland alongside a deeply incised stream down to a small gateway. Go through it and walk by the remains of an old kissing gate, and you'll see houses to your right. The path leads though a hedge to the left and over a footbridge to another kissing gate. Go through this to a track with a three pronged sign. Go through another kissing gate ahead and then bear slightly left, diagonally up the field to a stile. Cross this and then turn right onto a well worn path leading downhill to Llandrindod Wells' charming boating lake.

At the lakeside bear right for the short walk into the town and to the railway station in the town centre.

Walk 11: The Vale of Rheidol

Landranger Map: Sheet 135.

Pathfinder Map: Sheet 947 (SN67/77).
(See also the excellent series of Walkers' maps from Aberystwyth and stations on the Rheidol Valley Railway issued by the Tourism Department of Ceredigion District Council and available from the Tourist Office, address below. There is a charge.)

Starting Station: Rheidol Falls.

Finishing Station: Devil's Bridge (Vale of Rheidol Railway).

Distance: 5 miles (8 km).

Time required: $2^1/2$ - 3 hours but allow plenty of time to explore Devil's Bridge Falls.

Grade: Moderate - one steep climb.

Possible Cut-off Point: Rhiwfron (request stop) $3^1/2$ miles (5 km).

Terrain: mainly woodland paths.

Refreshment and Accommodation: Aberystwyth is a major resort with excellent choice of accommodation and facilities. Cafes, shops, pub, some overnight accommodation at Devil's Bridge. Cafeteria at Devil's Bridge Station. Youth Hostel at Ystumtuen, two miles from Devil's Bridge Station.

Tourist Information: Eastgate, Aberystwyth, Dyfed, SY23 2AR. Tel.(0970) 612125/611955.

THE RAIL JOURNEY

The main Cambrian Line from Machynlleth to Aberystwyth may lack something of the scenic grandeur of the Cambrian Coast Line which forks away northwards at Dovey Junction - a station with no road access. It is nonetheless an extremely pleasant journey with some good coastal scenery before you arrive at Aberystwyth's handsome Victorian station. If you've time to explore the town with its grand seafront terraces, make your way to see and preferably travel on its remarkable Cliff Railway - the longest funicular railway in Britain, which leads to the town's Camera Obscura.

The Vale of Rheidol Railway is also something quite extraordinary. This $11^1/_2$ mile long line was built to a 1 foot $11^1/_2$ inches gauge, yet has heavy little steam engines weighing a full 25 tons. It was opened in 1902 to serve local leadmines and for timber, but also with an eye on the local tourist trade from the resort of Aberystwyth to Devil's Bridge. Its particular claim to fame is that it was also the last British Rail line to be operated by steam, remaining in B.R. ownership until 1988 before someone in B.R. finally decided to call a halt to nostalgia. At the time of writing the line is in the process of being "privatised".

This is very much a valley line, beginning in the flat valley bottom of the Afon Rheidol, paralleling the Cambrian Line so that you may see an elderly steam train and a high speed modern Sprinter train running side by side.

The really serious work doesn't begin until Capel Bangor, where the regulators open and the little engines have to bark their way up the valley sides rapidly gaining height to Nantyronen. They then follow a narrow shelf up and above the valley floor, soon entering dense woodland, high above a deep, narrow valley of almost Alpine proportions, with splendid views from the little carriages - so sit on the left hand side if you can. If you are alighting at any of the halts, including Rheidol Falls for this walk, alert the guard at Aberystwyth otherwise the train won't stop, except for water at Nantyronen, until it pulls into Devil's Bridge Station.

THE WALK

Don't expect a conventional station when the train wheezes to a halt at Rheidol Falls - a station name plate and trackside pine needles are all that will greet you as you climb down from the Continental style carriages which do not require conventional high platforms. There's also a sign to tell you that you are 380 feet above sea level, just about every foot of which the train has climbed. Sadly, you're about to lose much of this height on a descent to the valley bottom and Rheidol Falls.

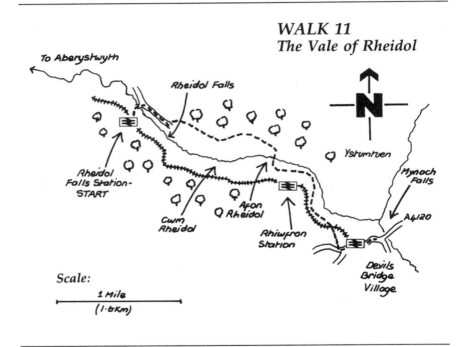

WALK 11
The Vale of Rheidol

To Aberystwyth

Rheidol Falls

Rheidol Falls Station-START

Cwm Rheidol

Afon Rheidol

Rhiwfron Station

Ystumtuen

Mynach Falls

A4120

Devils Bridge Village

Scale:

1 Mile
(1·6Km)

Rheidol Falls

Your way out of the station is a little pedestrian gate a few yards below the station in the Aberystwyth direction. This leads to a path deep into the forest, which winds slowly down to the left for 150 metres to a junction before zizagging right to a stile at the bottom of the wood. Cross this and go down to a stile by a picnic site near a metal footbridge over the river and a viewpoint for the little series of waterfalls and hydro-electric plant above. Notice the concrete "ladder" to allow salmon to pass the weir.

Continue along the path to a lane and little cottage. Turn right along the lane, looking across the valley to pick out the railway high above, perhaps with a tell-tale plume of steam from deep within the woods.

Coed Simdde Lwyd

Near a new farmhouse on the left, a footpath sign indicates a path through gates and alongside a stream. This leads to a little footbridge and steps, and a stile into a beautiful woodland nature reserve, Coed Simdde Lwyd. This is an ancient oak wood, with bilberry flourishing below the light covering of leaves.

Follow the path uphill, obliquely right, through the wood. As the gradient eases, paths cross - bear right here to a stile in the reserve fence. The path continues along the hillside, just above the boundary fence, curving round into the next side valley and descending slightly. Ignore the stile on the right, but cross the stream above the fence on the right. Climb for another 150 metres along a faint path by the stream until you eventually meet a wider track coming down from the left. Go right here following the track eastwards as it gradually descends past the ruins of a farm and a stream becoming a lovely greenway by old hedges and trees. Keep the same direction until it reaches the workings of Rheidol Mine, bending sharply round to reach the lane below the mines.

Lead and Silver Mines

The huge workings and spoil tips covering the hillside are a vivid reminder that this was an area once extensively mined for lead and silver. One of the mines, Llywernog Silver-Lead Mines, about three miles from here on the A44, has been opened as a major visitor centre with exhibition areas and restored machinery.

Below is Pontbren Falls and footbridge. Cross the bridge to a gate, turning left up the slope to a stile, and keeping ahead to a pedestrian gate. There is an extensive view of the mines across the valley as you climb. Go over another stile into the wood. Keep ahead now along a well walked path which gradually slopes upwards into the wood and soon becomes a narrow way between the trees and clumps of bilberry. It continues to ascend, a real Alpine path. Keep ahead as you approach the railway line above until the path eventually leads you up some steps onto the railway track at a stile. Turn left.

The public path now follows the railway line for some 80 metres through a narrow cutting across a steep gorge. Stop, look and listen and only if you are quite certain no train is coming (the whistle and the panting of the engines will give you about three minutes' warning) proceed quickly to reach another white painted stile on the left.

National Nature Reserve

The path now goes below the railway - look for waymarks - through another lovely section of natural woodland, Coed Rheidol National Nature Reserve with sessile oak, holly and ash. The path swings back to the railway, this time crossing through gates and bearing left to a stile, and climbing up a low knoll above the line from where there are fine views across surrounding hills.

You soon reach a track which turns right across a field to a gate by a white bungalow on the main A4120 just above Devil's Bridge.

Devil's Bridge

Turn left. Five minutes' walk down the road will bring you to Devil's Bridge Station; another three minutes' walk to the series of cataracts, reached through a turnstile - small fee payable - and down a series of steps to where the River Mynach, a tributary of the Rheidol, thrusts and fumes its way through a narrow gorge.

There are actually three bridges here, each built across the other, - the lowest reputedly built by the Devil himself. Legend has it that many years ago an old woman's cow was stranded on the far bank and Old Nick offered to build a bridge if he could have the soul of the first living being to cross. He imagined the old woman would oblige when she went to fetch her cow. He had not reckoned with the natural sharpness of Welsh ladies. She first threw over a morsel of bread which her little dog chased after, then she reclaimed her cow, so the Devil had to make do with the soul of a dog.

Devil's Bridge Falls

Walk 12: Cocklers' ways: Kidwelly to Ferryside

Landranger Map: Sheet 159.

Pathfinder Maps: Sheets 1105 and 1106, (SN40/50 SN20/30).

Starting Station: Kidwelly.

Finishing Station: Ferryside (B.R. Table 128).

Distance: 5 miles (9 km).

Time Required: $2^1/_2$ hours.

Grade: Easy.

Possible Cut-Off Point: No suitable point.

Terrain: Estuarine landscape then mainly across rich pastureland with good views across Carmarthen Bay and the Afon Tywi to Dylan Thomas Country.

Refreshment and Accommodation: Available at Kidwelly, Llansaint and Ferryside. Youth Hostel at Port Eynon on Gower.

Tourist Information: Lammas Street, Carmarthen, Dyfed. SA31 3AQ Tel: (0267) 231557, or Singleton Street, Swansea, West Glamorgan. SA1 3QN Tel: (0792) 468321.

THE RAIL JOURNEY

It was the endeavours of the South Wales Railway Company in the early 1850s that led to the building of the present railway between Swansea and Carmarthen. The main intention was to seek out a suitable port for traffic to Ireland. At first, Neyland, then known as 'New Milford' was developed and it was much later that plans for Pembroke and Fishguard came to fruition. The terminus at Fishguard, for example, was not completed until 1906, well into the era of the Great Western Railway.

The Gower

Most trains travelling to West Wales either call or start at Swansea and then travel by way of Llanelli to Kidwelly. Not all of them stop at Kidwelly and Ferryside so choose your timings carefully. Swansea is a fine university town, much rebuilt after the Second World War and is now redeveloping part of its dockland for leisure purposes. It is the nearest access point for the Gower Peninsula, a designated Area of Outstanding Natural Beauty with several excellent beaches fit for the most enthusiatic sand castle builder as well as miles of dramatic cliff scenery for lovers of fine seascape. The world's first passenger carrying railway, the Mumbles Railway, operated between Swansea and Oystermouth as early as 1807 but sadly closed some time ago. Not surprisingly the peninsula and coastline are popular places at weekends but this walk avoids the more popular areas, to explore some delightful yet quiet countryside by the River Tywi.

The railway line from Swansea to Llanelli passes Loughor where there are views of the castle to the right and of the Gower to the left, including the village of Penclawdd where cockles are still collected. This part of the Gower has also traditionally been associated with the collection of seaweed for the production of laver bread, a Welsh delicacy which can still be enjoyed in these parts.

Shipwrecks

Beyond Llanelli, a town celebrated for its tinplate factories and breweries, the views from the carriage window begin to open up and as the train approaches Pembrey and Burry Port unusual-looking windmills can be seen alongside the disused power station. At this point you also begin to see a vast expanse of forest along the coastline. This is Pembrey Country Park. At low tide it is possible to see the remains of wrecked boats on the Cefn Sidan sands reflecting not only the dangerous tidal conditions but also the activities of smugglers in earlier times.

Kidwelly

This small community, which lies nearly half way between Carmarthen and Llanelli, has grown up partly as a consequence of its potential as a port, which the invading Normans took advantage of when building their castle, but more so in recent times as a producer of tinplate.

Kidwelly Castle

The castle dominates the skyline. The Norman onslaught against the Welsh kingdoms began shortly after the Conquest in the latter part of the eleventh century. Kidwelly was one of the castles built at a strategic seashore location along with Manorbier, Pembroke and Cardigan. If the defending Welsh regained inland areas, supplies and reinforcements could still be brought in by sea to such garrisons in order to re-assert control.

Kidwelly Castle was almost certainly built during the reign of Henry I in the early part of the 12th century. Its construction exemplifies the thoroughness of the Norman overlords in defensive strategy, for it is sited on a ridge on the west bank of the Gwendraeth Fach at the upper limit of its tidal section.

The Castle is now in the possession of CADW, Welsh Historic Monuments, and is open to the public throughout the year. There is an excellent guide book to the Castle outlining key features of interest and you will need a good two hours to do justice to everything there is to see. There is also a small tinplate museum, the Kidwelly Tinplate Works, situated about a mile from Kidwelly off the Mynydd y Garreg road.

THE WALK

Leave the station platform and once clear of the level crossing turn right by the Anthony Hotel then left towards the centre of Kidwelly. Turn left into Bridge Street, now heading towards the castle. Opposite 'Country Antiques' and the Steam Bakery there is a footpath signed to the left by Trinity Chapel. This recently improved way follows the Gwendraeth Fach through a marshy area to a tarmac road. On the opposite banks there used to be a small port served by a railway, now dismantled, which brought tinplate to ships for despatch to other parts of the country.

Cockles

Turn left here and walk along this road until you reach an old farm on the left known as Penallt. Bear right here up a beautifully secluded track to the village of Llansaint. This was probably one of the routes used by Llansaint women and their donkeys making their way down to the shores of the Gwendraeth Fach to collect cockles. Llansaint has a strong tradition of this type of activity, which unfortunately no longer survives. It is an excellent place to stop for refreshments as there are two centrally situated inns in the village.

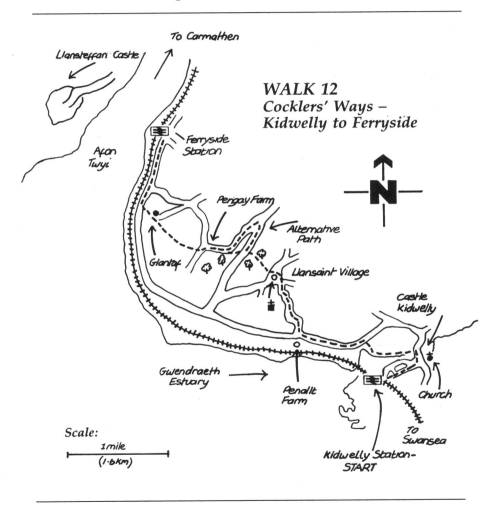

To Carmarthen

Llansteffan Castle

Ferryside Station

Afon Twyi

WALK 12
*Cocklers' Ways –
Kidwelly to Ferryside*

N

Pengay Farm

Alternative Path

Glanlof

Llansaint Village

Castle Kidwelly

Gwendraeth Estuary

Penallt Farm

Church

To Swansea

Kidwelly Station – START

Scale:
1 mile
(1·6km)

Turn left and in the village turn right then left. Your way ahead is a lane leading gently downwards between a farm and house opposite a chapel.The track is signed as a footpath. This track soon leads out into a field by way of a stile next to a barred gate. Continue slightly right to a stile in the hedge opposite. Cross this and continue downhill, with the hedge to your left at first. The path then leads off to the right towards the small sewerage works. A gate leads down to a tarmac lane.

Opposite the works there is a narrow path crossing a hidden bridge into the woodland. Follow this up through the wood to a stile. Cross this and walk slightly left, keeping the hedge to your left, up to the top left hand corner of the field where a barred gate leads onto the tarmac road. The path in the wood can become overgrown and is eroding in places so if at an early stage you find it difficult then there is an easier alternative. At the sewerage works, go right along the tarmac lane and at the T junction bear left.

Llansteffan Castle

Either way, you should now be on the tarmac lane leading to Pengay Farm. At the triangle bear left but do not then turn left again. Continue ahead through a gateway. Walk ahead with the field boundary to your right to another gateway. Continue ahead once again. You might see the trig point in the next field on your right. From this superb viewpoint you can now see Llansteffan Castle and beyond into 'Dylan Thomas Country'. The castle, like Kidwelly, is situated on a defensive bluff on a peninsula between the Afon Taf and Afon Tywi. This 13th century Norman outpost, the seat of the de Camvilles family, is open to the public and access is by way of the sleepy village of Llansteffan.

Dylan Thomas

Dylan Thomas could not have described the area better when he referred to nearby Laugharne as a 'timeless, mild, beguiling island of a town' and the surrounding villages and towns reflect these sentiments. He captured the Welshness of this countryside and its people so well in short stories such as 'The Peaches'. Dylan Thomas is buried in Laugharne, and The Boathouse where he spent a number of years writing before his death in 1953 is open to the public.

With a gentle breeze on your face follow the indistinct path down to a gateway and you will see a pool on the left and a house, Glantaf, to the right. Bear right, heading for the next gateway and then across the next field towards Glantaf. The right of way is in this field corner. A tree has been removed and new drainage provided. There is no stile and it is quite a drop to the track below but the way is not obstructed.

Cross the track to the opposite corner and make your way down the path between hedges to the left of the house. This leads down to a stream and then a stile, both of which you cross. Continue down the valley with the stream to your left. Go over the next stile beneath the tree and then continue ahead to the next hedgerow where there is no proper stile. The easiest way through is over an old iron gate. The path continues down to the wood to a stile slightly to the left which resembles a diving board.The way becomes much clearer again and is fenced most of the way down to the road. It is steep in places and the iron steps should be negotiated with caution as they are in a poor state of repair.

Ferryside

At the tarmac road bear right and then at the next junction left. The road descends and continues into the centre of Ferryside where you will find the railway station. In the summer the cafe is usually open and there are two conveniently situated public houses near the station. The village grew up as its the name suggests as the point on the Tywi Estuary where the ferry crossed for Llansteffan. Sadly, this last operated in 1948 and the journey now has to be made the long way round by way of Carmarthen. The settlement also survived by fishing and, like Llansaint, engaged in cockle collecting. With the coming of the railways in the 1850s, a small seaside resort grew up; although bathing in the strong tidal waters has always been dangerous, this is an area of great appeal to yachtsmen.

Walk 13: West Cleddau

Landranger Map: Sheet 158.

Pathfinder Map: Sheet 1079 (SM 81/9).

Starting Station: Johnston.

Finishing Station: Haverfordwest (B.R. Table 128).

Distance: 7 miles (11 km).

Time Required: 3 to 4 hours.

Grade: Easy to Moderate.

Possible Cut-off Point: The walk can be shortened by catching a bus from Haverfordwest to Freystop, avoiding some road walking.

Terrain: Gentle landscapes with very few gradients to encounter. Some road walking but some lovely stretches of footpath in the latter part of the walk to compensate.

Refreshment and Accommodation: Shops are available at Johnston. The only refreshment spot en route is the New Anchor public house at Hook. There is a plentiful supply of cafes, shops, and accommodation of all grades at Haverfordwest.

Tourist Information: 40 High Street, Haverfordwest, Dyfed SA62 6SD. Tel. (0837) 3110.

THE RAIL JOURNEY

The railway line to Milford Haven branches from the Fishguard line at Clarbeston Road and runs through pleasant dairy farming countryside to Haverfordwest and on to Milford Haven. It was the South Wales Railway Company's original route to Ireland, the port being opened in

1853, well before before Fishguard Harbour which was only built many years later by the Great Western Railway.

The entire journey beyond Llanelli is full of interest as you pass by sleepy villages and distant farmsteads, crossing estuaries and stopping at junction stations.

THE WALK

From Johnston railway station turn left, right at the main A4076 road then first left along the road signposted to Llangwm. Johnston is not, perhaps, a particularly attractive place to linger, so proceed quickly along this road, which has quite a bit of traffic, for about a mile to a cross roads. Bear left for Targate along a much quieter lane. There is a more direct, and traffic-free, route by public footpath, but at the time of writing there were some obstructions. The path actually runs beyond Langford Farm through to Targate. The way goes through a barred gate on the left leading into a field which is usually under crop. The route is across this field bearing slightly left to a point mid field in the boundary hedge opposite and continuing along the next field hedge up to Cranham farm and onto a tarmac lane at Targate. The main obstruction is the very thick hedge without a stile. Most people will probably prefer the road as an easier option.

Hook

Whichever way you come, you must follow the road, noting the old agricultural implements to the left, from Targate to Freystop. At Freystop crossroads continue ahead and the road winds down to Maddox Moor and Hook. The road bends down to the right by Little Milford wood and the New Anchor public house is on the left. Hook was once a mining area and had in fact the last anthracite mine in Pembrokeshire to close. Anthracite is a high quality, low smoke fuel once much sought after for ship and locomotive boilers - and Welsh anthracite was the best in the world. Much of the coal was shipped out from the quayside which still remains.

Retrace your steps a short distance to join a path leading off to the right (or your left if you decide not to call at the pub), between two bungalows, into the wood. This beautiful path links up shortly with another, where you bear right. It leads down to a stile near a farm building. Turn left here and then right at the next junction passing by Little Milford. Go right across a marshy section and cross the stream. Take the lower path, closest to the estuary and waymarked in yellow.

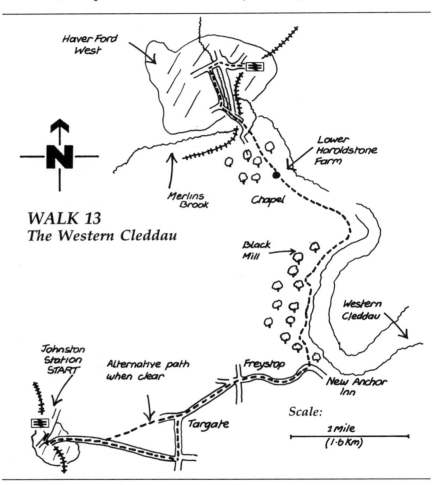

The Western Cleddau

This is an exquisite stretch of waterway which meets the Eastern Cleddau to become the Milford Haven. It is geologically speaking a *ria*, a river eroded valley flooded as a consequence of a rising sea level. The waterway is rich in birdlife and at most times is incredibly quiet.

Go over a stile, still keeping to the edge of the wood and estuary. Cross a small stream and at this point the path splits, going either along the higher level fields or along the estuary. Either way you pass by an old quarry and come to another stile waymarked yellow again. Pass by some old buildings and the path turns left then right to a gate. You then cross a footbridge and follow a path at the wood's edge. Go over a stile and walk upwards gently into the wood. The path becomes less well defined here but you should keep as close as possible to the edge nearest to the estuary.

The path now opens out into pastureland beneath Fern Hill farm. Follow the line of trees along the river's edge and as this curves left you will come across a stile on your left leading into a field once again. Cross it and bear right along the field boundary to another stile leading into a wood. The path falls slowly then climbs up, following the waymarks on the trees, to another stile. Cross it and turn right to the next stile. Go over this and proceed slightly left to the next stile. Go right here and downwards to yet another stile and then through a barred gate.

Bear right just before a chapel and then go left over a stile. Continue ahead along the line of trees and go through the gorse cover. Cross the footbridge and stile. The path leads up leftwards to a hedge on a bluff above the river. Go right here and follow along the bluff. The path begins to descend and then you go over a stile on the left only to turn right and follow the hedge on the other side. Haverfordwest is now 15 minutes' walk away. The path goes right then sharp left through a barred gate and over a stile to a tarmac lane. Go right here over the bridge, with Merlin's Brook beneath - no doubt some Pembrokeshire link with Arthurian legend.

The road leads over the railway and then climbs up to a junction. Go right and follow this to the old quayside area and the town centre to the left.

Haverfordwest

Haverfordwest is the old County town of Pembrokeshire and still retains an air of importance. It was a bridging point on the Western Cleddau and at one time had a thriving quayside. The Normans built a castle here about 1100 as part of a chain of castles across Pembrokeshire. They encircled the town with defensive walls to protect the English and Norman invaders and settlers against attacks from the Welsh to the north, helping to create Pembrokeshire as "a little piece of England beyond Wales". Little remains of either structure, the castle having been destroyed by Oliver Cromwell in the Civil War. The Castle Museum is housed in the remains. The main shopping streets are High Street and Bridge Street and there are numerous interesting buildings in the vicinity as well as a good choice of pubs and cafes. Saturday is market day; early closing is on Thursdays.

The railway station is to the right, across a busy roundabout and then signed off Cartlett Road - the A40 Carmarthen road.

Walk 14: Along the Pembrokeshire coast

Landranger: Sheet 158.

Pathfinder Map: Sheet 1126 (SS09/19).

Starting Station: Manorbier.

Finishing Station: Tenby (B.R. Table 128).

Distance: 9 miles (15km).

Time Required: Allow at least five hours.

Grade: Strenuous.

Possible Cut-Off Point: Lydstep - 4 miles (6.5 km), where a bus can be caught to Tenby or Penally railway station - 7 miles (11 km).

Terrain: Mainly coastal path but with some very steep climbs. Narrow in places. Requires care.

Refreshment and Accommodation: Cafes, shops, pubs, guest house and hotel accommodation in Manorbier, Lydstep and Tenby. There is a Youth Hostel in Manorbier.

Tourist Information: Guildhall, Tenby, Dyfed. Tel: (0834) 2402/3510; Canolfan Hywel Dda, Whitland, Dyfed, SA34 0PY. Tel: (0934) 240867.

THE RAIL JOURNEY

The journey from Cardiff, capital of Wales, to this land of magic and mystery is without doubt a varied one, but it is not until the train sweeps into Ferryside and the Tywi estuary that the scenery really attracts attention, not because it is dramatic but because of its green and gentle pastures. At Whitland the line to Pembroke Dock branches off to Narberth and Tenby. It then turns inland once again at Manorbier, the station being over a mile or a good 2 kilometres from the village itself.

Manorbier

Manorbier Castle, the birthplace of the 12th century scholar Gerald of Wales, is a landmark of significance. This medieval fortress, situated between the village and beach, was established by the de Barri family. It is now open to the public at certain times. Legend has it that one of the towers was used for storing contraband in later centuries. Manorbier, along with dozens of other Welsh seaside communities, indulged in smuggling on quite a scale. The isolation of the communities meant that the earlier version of the Customs and Excise men could not get to the scene of the crime quickly enough to apprehend the culprits. In some instances it would probably have meant arresting at least half the village!

The church opposite the castle dates mainly from the 12th century and must have been a church of worship for the garrison at some stage. This nine mile walk takes in a section of the Pembrokeshire Coastal Path, one of the most popular of Britain's coastal Long Distance Routes, which offer some fine cliff and shore scenery.

THE WALK

On leaving the platform of Manorbier station turn right to walk over the railway track at the crossing - stop to look and listen first - and then follow the lane to the main A4139 road, passing by a holiday and garden centre. At the junction cross over and walk down the drive signed to Norton Farm. As this track curves towards the farm your way is left over a stile leading into a field. Follow the field boundary around to a stile opening out onto a tarmac lane with a caravan park opposite. Bear right at first but not very far along take a turning to the left signed to Park Farm. Go down this pleasant valley and as the road veers to the right bear left across a grassy section to a lane leading left. Make sure you follow the tree clad path downwards in the direction of Manorbier Castle. Go over a stile and with the castle immediately on your right, then cross another stile into another wooded section with surrounding ruins. Climb up to a lane leading to the main entrance of the castle.

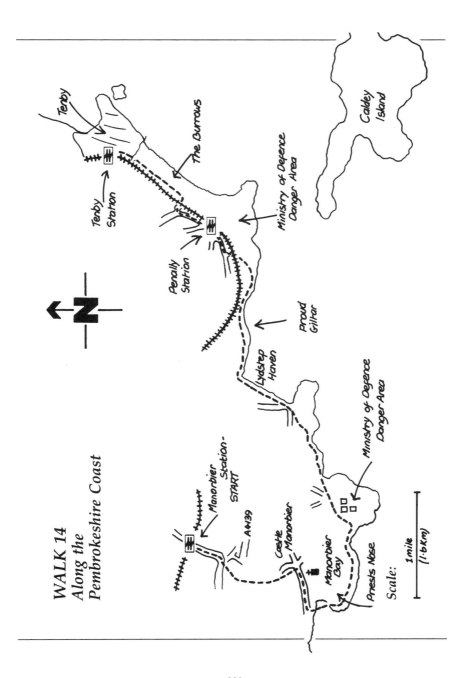

WALK 14
Along the
Pembrokeshire Coast

N

Tenby

The Burrows

Tenby Station

Penally Station

Ministry of Defence Danger Area

Caldey Island

Proud Gilrar

Lydstep Haven

Manorbier Station - START

A4139

Castle Manorbier

Ministry of Defence Danger Area

Manorbier Bay

Priests Nose

Scale:

1 mile
(1·6 km)

The Coastal Path

Unless you are visiting the castle during its opening hours turn left to meet the tarmac road. Manorbier is a pleasant enough village, twinned with Vernon-La Celle Sur Seine, France, and should you be in need of provisions or light refreshments then bear left. If not, turn right and walk down to the beach, turning left after the car park. Bear left along the beach and the coastal path can be picked up by walking up the concrete steps and crossing the stile. There is a considerable climb now up to Priest's Nose passing near to the primitive King's Quoit burial chamber. From Priest's Nose there are views along the coast to nearby Swanlake and Freshwater bays.

Coastal Footpath at Manorbier

The fissures to your right are quite spectacular but do not venture too close as this section is potentially very dangerous. Follow the well trodden path along the coast until you come to the first of a series of yellow markers directing you around the Ministry of Defence premises here. Go to the perimeter fence, bear left, then go over the next stile and bear right. Continue ahead over another stile following the perimeter fence to a stile leading to an access road. Cross this and go right and left and then right again, following the signpost to Shrinkle Haven. Proceed through a concrete area and then go left rather than continuing to Shrinkle Beach.

Lydstep Haven

Just beyond the sewerage works the path forks. Follow the lower cliff edge path. Once again the path becomes easy to follow with superb views of the coastline and a first glimpse of Caldey Island. There's a very strenuous set of steps up towards Lydstep. Go left at the top avoiding the turning right to Lydstep Point. The path leads to a lane. Go right down it to Lydstep Beach, hemmed in by caravans and chalets.

Caldey Island

The view of the Haven and Caldey Island is far more promising. Caldey Island lies three miles off the Pembrokeshire Coast. It was known in Celtic times as 'Ynys Pyr' after a ruling abbott, but the later Norse name, Caldey, 'The island of the Fresh Water Spring', seems to have persisted. Monks have lived on the island for over 1500 years and the present monastery was built in 1912. During the season visitors are ferried to Caldey and can see the work of the Monastery. However, only men can actually be allowed inside the Monastery!
Walk along the pebbly beach and at the far end you'll see the path rising up relentlessly towards the cliff tops once again. Be very careful towards Proud Giltar point as there are a number of gaping holes close to the path.

Penally

Nevertheless, the path is clear enough and once again you come to Ministry of Defence property. After reading several notices about the possibilty of being blown to bits on your afternoon ramble it seems sensible to follow the waymarked path to the main A4139 road at Penally. Tenby comes into sight and there's less than an hour's walking to the town centre. At the kissing gate go left and keep to the perimeter fence downhill to the railway. Follow the track to the main road and turn right. Walk along the verge to Penally station where there is a cafe and nearby public house should you be in need of refreshment.

Continue along the road for a short section and as it begins to curve to the left you go right along a track to the railway. Cross the track with care and once over go left. This takes you to the edge of the golf course and into Tenby. The station is directly ahead. The seafront and shops are signposted from this point.

Tenby

Tenby has long looked to the sea for its existence. The Welsh name for the town is 'Dinbych-y-Pysgod' meaning 'The little fort of the fishes'. There is still a small fishing fleet sailing from the harbour but pleasure craft are more in evidence. The castle, the ruins of which are to be seen on Castle Hill, was of significance as a coastal defence. Tenby Museum, displaying local exhibits, is partly housed in the castle buildings. Much of the old town is surrounded by walls dating back to the 13th century but considerably strengthened in the 16th century in anticipation of a Spanish invasion.

The town contains many fine Georgian buildings as well as the Tudor Merchant's House dating from the 15th and 16th centuries. The house is open to the public and exhibits many furnishings from different periods.

Tenby is a splendid destination for those who wish to explore the surrounding parts of old Pembrokeshire as well as dip their toes into the inviting water.

Walk 15: Three castles - Cardiff, Castell Coch, Caerphilly

Landranger Map: Sheet 171.

Pathfinder: 1148, 1165 (ST 08/18. ST17/27).

Starting Station: Cardiff Central.

Finishing Station: Caerphilly (B.R. Table 130).

Distance: 12 miles (19km).

Time required: 6 hours.

Grade: Moderate.

Possible cut off point: Radyr Station (6 miles); Taff's Well (8^1/$_2$ miles).

Terrain: Riverside tracks and paths, forest tracks, some fieldpaths.

Refreshment and Accommodation facilities: Cardiff, Caerphilly. Shops and pubs in Tongwynlais. Youth Hostel at LLwynypia (Rhondda).

Tourist Information: 8-14 Bridge Street, Cardiff, CF5 2EJ. Tel: (0222) 27281. The Old Police Station, Park Lane, Caerphilly, Mid Glamorgan, CF8 1AA. Tel: (0222) 863378.

THE RAIL JOURNEY

Anyone travelling to Cardiff from England has an interesting rail journey, either through the Severn Tunnel and along the Severn Estuary via Newport from London, Birmingham and Bristol, or down the scenic Marches Line from Crewe, Hereford and Abergavenny.

Cardiff is the focal point of the Valley Lines. These form a dense network of urban routes through the deep and narrow valleys which radiate from Cardiff down to the coast. Modern Sprinter trains operating every few minutes - most lines have a 30 minute service - make travel up and down the Valleys remarkably easy. They also make this an excellent area to walk in, in the confidence that even if you don't complete the full walk there's always a station not too far away with a train to take you quickly and easily back into Cardiff.

Cardiff

Cardiff is a great city, a true capital, with some impressive national and civic buildings, and you might well want to spend some time here before or after the walk. The most notable of these are Cathays Park - an area of magnificent Portland stone public buildings and gardens, including the National Museum of Wales, the shopping centre with pedestrian precincts and a delightful series of arcades. The Welsh Folk Museum is at St. Fagan's on the outskirts of the city, whilst another museum not to be missed is the Welsh Industrial and Maritime Museum at West Bute Dock.

Despite its size and importance as a city, Cardiff is a surprisingly green city and you can follow a fascinating riverside and woodland route directly from Bute Park in the heart of Cardiff city centre.

THE WALK

From Central Station cross directly past the bus station, turning right into Wood Street and left along Westgate Street to Cardiff Castle.

Cardiff Castle and Bute Park

If you've time, this, the first of the three Castles on this route, is well worth visiting. The Romans built a fort here, and this was followed by a great Norman castle on the site, but the present building, almost completely rebuilt and restored, was the work of the great Victorian architect William Burges for the third Marquis of Bute. Whilst the medieval keep is retained (and even a section of Roman wall is visible) this is now a palace of richly decorated interiors, and houses a major regimental museum.

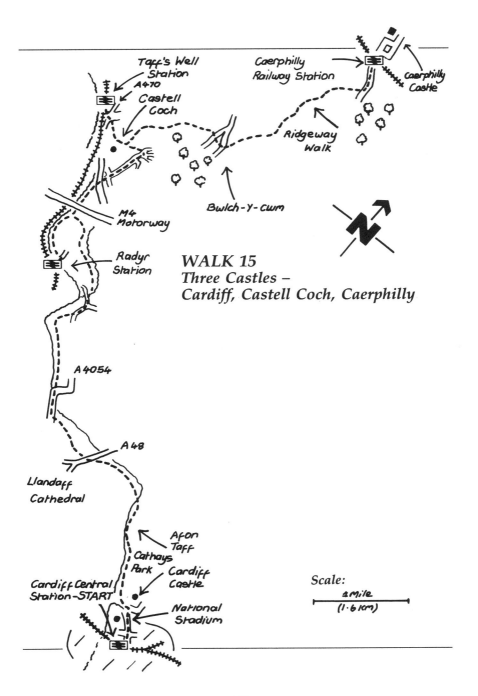

Taff's Well Station
A470
Castell Coch

Caerphilly Railway Station
Caerphilly Castle

Ridgeway Walk

Bulch-y-cwm

M4 Motorway

Radyr Station

WALK 15
Three Castles –
Cardiff, Castell Coch, Caerphilly

A4054

A48

Llandaff Cathedral

Afon Taff
Cathays Park
Cardiff Castle

Cardiff Central Station-START

National Stadium

Scale:
1 mile
(1·6 km)

117

The walk actually starts in the park - Bute Park - which is reached from the entrance past the splendidly carved walls of the castle. Make your way to the riverside and follow the River Taff upstream past the gardens and shrubbery of the park. As the park finally thins out the path becomes more rural in character,a thin strip of countryside coming to the very heart of the city.

Cross the narrow suspension bridge by a weir and turn right through a metal squeezer stile through a wooded area, continuing up river towards the handsome stone bridge which carries the busy A48 trunk road around Cardiff. Bear left to a gate and keep to the left of the wide grassy verge to reach the high metal footbridge which provides the only safe way across the main road to the South Glamorgan Institute of Higher Education on the other side. Keep in the same direction past a rugby clubhouse, then turn right along a tarmac way with a No Cycling sign between fences. This leads to Llandaff Cathedral.

Llandaff Cathedral

Llandaff Cathedral was founded by St. Teilo in the sixth century, but the present Cathedral dates from Norman times. Tragically, the Cathedral was gutted in an air-raid in 1941 but has been carefully restored, its most striking feature being Sir Jacob Epstein's magnificent "Christ in Majesty" which dominates the nave.

Just above the Cathedral, to the left, are the 800 year old remains of the Bishop's Palace, now converted to a small public garden.

Your way from the Cathedral entrance is to go sharp right (avoiding the enticing steps ahead) along a tarmac path. Follow it as it turns left to the embankment at another weir before climbing to the road at a kissing gate. Go right here, and almost immediately right again - this part of the route uses a section of the Taff Vale Heritage Trail and you'll see the wooden waymarks. The path leads to the riverside again, soon rejoining the road near the road bridge over the River Taff. Cross the bridge, keeping on the same side of the road to where steps, at the far side of the bridge, take you back down to the river and a path (not shown on the maps) underneath the bridge and along the riverside. This is Hailey Park - a pleasant open space by the Taff.

Continue up stream to the railway embankment where the path turns left to a bridge under the line. Follow the path left here into a small car park. Keep the same direction to pick up a narrow path ahead which dives down to a short tunnel beneath the next railway track to the right. You are now in a new housing estate. Keep ahead to the road junction ahead turning left to a fork at a white house where you bear right.

The Glamorgan Canal

Look for a metal gap stile and bridleway sign on the left - the path goes parallel to the lane, above an area of new development, soon re-emerging on the lane.

Now look for a stile on the right. This leads to the Glamorgan Canal Local Nature Reserve - a section of canal towpath along the disused Glamorgan Canal. This is a delightful stretch of waterway between the canal and the feeder to the former Melingriffith Mill. Keep on the old towpath until it ends abruptly at old locks below a road embankment; ahead a massive motorway complex carries the M4. Turn right past the Amersham International Factory back to the riverside. If you turn left the path leads to a footbridge at Radyr Station.

Castell Coch

The main route continues up river, this time going under the M4 and into a narrow gorge where river, railway and the A470 trunk road all compete for space. On the wooded hillside ahead, high above the gorge, you'll see the fairy-tale towers of Castell Coch.

Follow the path until it swings sharply right to a kissing gate by a white cottage, Ivy House Farm, and into Market Street. At the road junction you'll find two pubs and shops. Keep straight ahead up Mill Street, signed for Castell Coch, which you'll find after about half a mile walk uphill. Turn left up the steep drive through woods to the Castle itself, which is open daily. It's also a magnificent viewpoint from the woods across Taff Vale below.

Castell Coch is an architectural jewel, a delightful 19th century folly, built between 1875 and 1891 by the Marquis of Bute on the site of a 13th century ruin. Once again the design is by William Burges, this time in the form of a Swiss medieval castle, all turrets and towers, a pastiche perhaps but executed enchantingly with a little courtyard surrounded by a series of rooms richly decorated in Pre-Raphaelite style.

Castell Coch

It is sad to reflect that this little pleasure palace was seldom used. However, it remains an exquisite piece of architectural fantasy, a kind of miniature Neuschwanstein high in the wooded hills above the Taff.
If you want to return to Cardiff, a steep and not too easy footpath

behind the castle (it runs near the fence) leads down to the bottom of the woods where there is a stile. Ahead there is a traffic island. Cross by walking around the island and follow the road at the far side parallel to the railway line to the right. Here a path leads to the road over the bridge into Taff's Well and Taff's Well Station on the right.

Forest walk

For the final part of the walk into Caerphilly, return to the castle drive, but about 30 metres along the drive look for a path which slopes uphill left - one of the Castles' Woodland Trails. This path broadens to a forest track. Keep the same direction at a crossing, climbing steadily along the straight track which, eventually, at the edge of the forest, Fforest-fawr, bends slightly right and begins to descend.

About a mile from Castell Coch the track emerges at a car park and picnic site above a lane. Turn right into the lane, looking for a stile and gate a few metres on the left. Go through here, following the track as it climbs through beechwoods, but look for a path which climbs left after 130 metres up a series of shallow steps to a stile at the lane above. Turn right here for about 200 metres, before turning left onto a signposted track below Bwlch y Cwm farm. Keep on the main track, ignoring a path right, straight ahead to the farmhouse and stables at Cefncarnau-fawr. Go through the gate past the stables, turning left up the side of the fence and hedge, climbing uphill. Keep the same direction through gates before bearing half right to the top of a low hill crowned by a scatter of trees. Slightly below and to the right a bridlegate marks the path. Approach it, but don't go through, keeping left of it to the hurdle stile. Cross, following the hedge to where a gate leads to the other side of the fence. Continue over a dip and a stream to the tarmac road by open moorland.

Caerphilly Mountain

Cross, heading for a clear, deep track across Caerphilly Common to the left. Follow this path along the edge of the moor but strike off along a path, left, which leads to the trig point at the summit of what is locally known as Caerphilly Mountain.

This is a another magnificent viewpoint, with the whole of Caerphilly spread out before you and in the centre, its massive Castle with its cluster of towers and great, grand moat.

Several ways and paths leave the summit. The best way into Caerphilly is to go straight ahead along a path which drops down steeply, turning right at the second crossing path. Pick up a path which descends to the bottom right hand corner of the common where another path fords (slightly awkwardly) a stream to reach the road into Caerphilly.

Caerphilly Castle

This road soon reaches Caerphilly Station with frequent trains back to Cardiff. But if you've another half mile in you, walk on into the little town centre to discover the largest castle in Wales - built by Gilbert de Clare, Earl of Gloucester in 1272. It really is an astonishing building, technically years ahead of its time and virtually impregnable, though that old magician Owain Glyndwr held it for a time against Henry IV. The fantastic leaning tower was caused by Oliver Cromwell's artillery in a later fracas.

Walk 16: The Rhondda Valley

Landranger Map: Sheet 170.

Pathfinder Maps: Sheets 1128, 1129, (SS89/99, SS09/19).

Starting Station: Porth.

Finishing Station: Ton Pentre (B.R. Table 130).

Distance: 7 miles (11 km).

Time required: $3^1/2$ hours.

Grade: Moderate - strenuous.

Possible cut off point: Penrhys for Ystrad Rhondda Station $4^1/2$ miles (7 km).

Terrain: Open moorland tracks and paths. Not recommended in poor visibility.

Refreshment and Accommodation: Pubs, cafes, shops in Porth and Ton Pentre. Limited accommodation in both towns - but Cardiff and Pontypridd easily accessible. There is a Youth Hostel at Llwynypia - about 1 mile from Ton Pentre near Llwynypia station.

Tourist Information: Bridge Street, Pontypridd, Mid Glamorgan CF37 4PE. Tel: (0443) 402077; 8-14 Bridge Street, Cardiff, CF5 2EJ. Tel: (0222) 27281.

THE RAIL JOURNEY

The Valley Lines of South Wales might well not merit inclusion in a scenic rail atlas - there's too much industry and industrial remains for that - but in between the steel works, the coal workings, the industrial estates and towns, lies an older Wales, a land of open rolling hills, deep craggy valleys, woods and forests. As industry retreats or takes new forms, many of the older derelict areas are recovering their former green mantle as replanting and restoration schemes reclaim the countryside. Both the rail journey and this particular walk will furnish dramatic contrasts of this nature - part of what the Welsh Valleys are all about.

This walk is on the Treherbert line from Cardiff which follows the Afon Taff through the narrow gorge of Taff Vale, past Castell Coch (see Walk 15). At the busy station of Pontypridd it branches into the Rhondda Valley itself, with views of crags and open moorland above the industry and terraced streets that crowd the valley floor and lower slopes.

Stanleytown, Rhondda Valley

THE WALK

Alight at Porth Station, and from the station road walk to and turn right into the main street through this busy little town. Keep on the Pontypridd road over the railway, but turn sharp left over the railway bridge heading to Ferndale road, past the Tynewydd Hotel to a mini roundabout. Cross to some stone steps immediately ahead, which climb behind the Ynyshir sign and eventually wind up to a terraced street ahead.

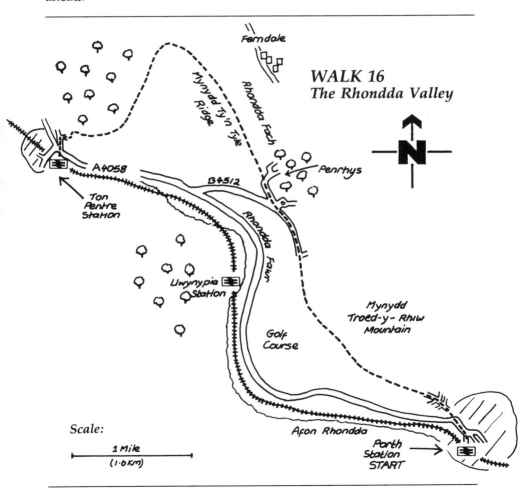

Two Rhondda valleys

Your way now climbs directly up the hillside through a steep little housing estate, then by a long, steep terrace of cottages where cobbles in the roadway evidently help horses to grip the steep surface. As the terraces end the road becomes a track heading due northwestwards through open countryside, soon reaching Troed-y-rhiw farm, which appears to farm mainly old cars for scrap. Do not go to the farm but look for a track which climbs up to your right, above and behind the farmhouse.

This is your route for the next mile, climbing slowly uphill along the broad ridge which separates the two Rhondda valleys - Rhondda Fach to the east and Rhondda Fawr to the west. You'll soon notice a massive graveyard below you - witness to the shortage of land in the valley bottom necessitating use of the hillside for this purpose. Beyond is the town of Tonypandy spreading up the hillside.

Exmoor views

As you ascend the hill of Mynydd Troed-y-rhiw you will come to a fork in the tracks. The more obvious way to the right is in fact a private farm track. Your way is the less clear route between fallen drystone walls. Keep ahead through a gate and continue alongside a fence. The next gate ahead leads to a golf course where you are requested to keep to the "Parish Road" - the public bridleway away from the fairways. You soon reach the summit of the ridge with a trig point which is a magnificent viewpoint. If the weather is clear you'll not only have a superb view across both Rhondda valleys but back towards Cardiff Bay and the Severn Estuary, and right across the estuary to the hills of Exmoor.

Keep ahead past the golf house and along the drive to the slightly incongruous Penrhys estate ahead. This is a modern housing estate in a superb situation over 1,000 feet above sea level but requiring a steep walk or minibus ride to or from the rest of the area. If you decide to end the walk here (advised if the weather if poor as the remainder of the walk is over open moorland with few landmarks) turn left downhill to Ystrad Rhondda Station, a recently reopened halt on the Treherbert line about a mile from Penrhys.

Brecon Beacons

Otherwise, your route is across the main road, the B4512, bearing right past a little park to pick up the road, left, which climbs around the outside rim of the housing estate. Follow the crash barrier as it curves uphill - a murderously steep climb which local people must frequently have to tackle with shopping.

Look for a rickety wooden stile on the left, near the top of the road. This gives access to the footpath which parallels the road, and goes through a gateway in the fence ahead towards a forestry plantation. This is an area which is clearly used by local children as a playgound, and their litter and detritus is all too clearly in evidence. At the plantation turn sharp left to take a path parallel to and outside the trees, continuing uphill.

This is a path which is not shown on the map but which crosses a great urban common - Mynydd Ty'n-tyle - to which there is public access. The path, clear on the ground, follows the ridge in a north-north westerly direction.

At this point the walk, pleasant enough so far, takes on a new dimension. Suddenly you are in a mountain landscape, wild and lonely - acres of open moorland, mountain top and forest. The summits of the Brecon Beacons appear in a cluster to the north.

Yet industry is not absent. To your right a waterfall above Ferndale is a mine drain, to your left pit shafts are evident.

Keep on this path as it follow the great ridge between the two valleys to a little summit and magnificent viewpoint. About a mile from Penrhyn the route begins to curve to the left and gradually descends, as you approach a wall on the right. You eventually reach an important crossing of five paths. The way you have been walking heads to the woodland, paths come up from Ferndale on the right, and two routes go down to Rhondda Fawr on the left.

Rhondda Fawr

Your route is not the way sharp left, but at about right angles along an old, deep sunken packhorse way, paved in places. which drops straight down the hillside. The path now edges around the top of a shallow Cwm or Corrie - Cwm Bodringallt. After about 300 metres this path again divides, one route, a bridleway, dropping down the valley to a gate below. Take the other path; this descends gradually to a gate, below left, then continues through the gate in the far corner of the next field. It carries on through an awkward area of rough land crossed by a mine drain or flue. Keep the same direction, nevertheless, through the gates. Your way is to contour round the edge, only losing height gradually. The landmark to look out for a large concrete archway over a stream overlooking a steep edge.

This is a superb vantage point to look across the Rhondda Valley, with the mines, the factories, the chapels, the characteristic lines of colour washed terraced houses set against the magnificent backcloth of hills and forest. To the right is Treorchy of Male Voice Choir fame, and beyond Treherbert at the head of the valley.

Your route down is to the right, a narrow path of which there are several (these hills are well walked by the people of the Rhondda) curving down the hillside - don't lose height too quickly, but look for a path that slopes into a track which zigzags to your left down by allotments and behind houses, into the main street of Pentre. Turn right to the station.

Walk 17: Along the Rhymney Valley Ridgeway

Landranger Map: Sheet 171.

Pathfinder Map: Sheet 1109 (SO 00/10).

Starting Station: Pontlottyn.

Finishing Station: Bargoed (B.R. Table 130).

Distance: 6 miles (9.5 km).

Time Required: Three Hours.

Grade: Moderate.

Possible Cut-off Point: Along Cefn-y-Brithdir to Tir-Phil after 2 miles (3^1/$_2$ km).

Terrain: A steep climb up to the moorland mountain above the Rhymney Valley. Mainly moorland paths and tracks.

Refreshment and Accommodation: Limited accommodation is available in the valley but there are shops and public houses at Pontlottyn and Bargoed. The latter also has cafes.

Tourist Information: Old Police Station, Caerphilly, Mid Glamorgan CF8 1AA. Tel: (0222) 863378; Bridge Street, Cardiff, CF5 2EJ. Tel: (0222) 27281.

THE RAIL JOURNEY

The Rhymney Valley, like its more famous neighbour the Rhondda, has been a mining valley, its railway primarily built to help win coal. Like the other Valley lines this is enjoying a remarkable revival thanks to the support and help of local authorities in the area, and it provides an excellent public transport service up and down the valley and to and from Cardiff.

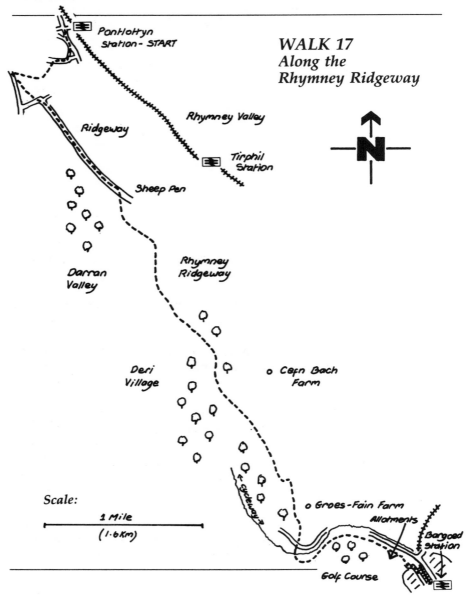

WALK 17
Along the
Rhymney Ridgeway

Like the Rhondda, too, the journey up the Rhymney Valley, whilst predominantly industrial, offers some superb stretches of open countryside above the densely populated and industrialised valley, a different world which is very accessible from the Valley line stations.

THE WALK

This short route uses part of one of several fine high-level ridge walks which are to be found between the Valleys - many of them using ancient tracks and green roads which date back many hundreds of years.

Pontlottyn

Pontlottyn is a small former mining community and the houses in the village are nestled around the rail and road links on the lower slopes of the valley. Like so many communities in South Wales it contains several chapels. Chapel has remained part of the way of life in the valleys, even though the numbers worshipping have fallen drastically in recent decades. The chapels grew in number during the last century. Many of them date back a hundred years though in some instances they are much older. The architectural styles vary from simple barn-like structures to ornate 'Gothic Revival' type buildings. There were several non-conformist denominations such as the Welsh Congregationalists, Presbyterians and Baptists. Not only did they form a place of worship for villagers but also a focal point for education and music. The local preachers were renowned for their oratory and many an aspiring teacher or politician no doubt learned much from the techniques of the local preacher. Pontlottyn retains some of its chapels and you pass by most of them as you walk through the village.

From the railway station platform walk to the main road in the village passing by the Empire Club. Cross the main road, turn left then go right onto the road signposted to Fochriw. Turn next left up Fochriw Road and as this begins to climb more steeply by a group of houses on the left you will see a footpath sign on the left just before a lost railway wagon on the roadside.

Go through the first kissing gate and head upwards to another kissing gate. Turn right here and follow the path to a tarmac lane. From here there are good views up the Rhymney valley. The landscape has changed considerably during the last two decades. It is not hard to imagine how this would have looked in the heyday of coal mining.

The Rhymney Valley Ridgeway

Turn left at the tarmac lane and then off to the left again along a path, which is waymarked, which climbs up to a rough track. You are now on the 'Rhymney Valley Ridgeway', a route developed by local authorities in the area principally for walkers and the views along it are extensive. It is a different world on the ridges above the valleys, a world which has been shaped little by man, a landscape which changed little during the period of heavy industry when iron and coal production so transformed the valleys. Cross to rejoin the tarmac lane once again.

The Darran Valley

Follow this quiet lane for some distance until you reach the moortop. You will see a dry stone wall belonging to a sheep pen on your left and a broken gate. At this point turn right across the moorland and into the bracken. This becomes a clearly defined path bearing to the left at first then slightly right alongside a fence descending gently to a stile. Cross over it and continue ahead. In the valley below you can see the effects of land reclamation, a walkway and cycle route using the old railway trackbed. This is part of the "greening" of the Darran Valley which is opening it up to a growing number of visitors. Further up the valley is Parc Cwm Darran, a country park based around a man-made lake and wooded hillsides.

Follow the path through the bracken to a main track leading upwards through the natural and ancient woodland on the valley side. This climbs up to a crossing of tracks where you turn right. Follow the clear track, through a small red gate by an exceedingly high drystone wall, and continue ahead, ignoring the track leading off to the left to Cefn Bach Farm. Proceed ahead through the next gate and keep ahead once again until you come to the next kissing gate. Go through it and keeping the drystone wall to the left, go through a gateway to the next field. You come across two gates and a stile. Choose the stile and then go left along a short section of green lane only to turn next right downhill. Cross the stile and go down another green lane.

Caerphilly Castle

Breathing space

A farm appears below you to the left and your path now begins to curve down, crossing a track and then continuing down another delightful walled green lane through a kissing gate to meet the farm track. Continue ahead downwards and as the lane curves right go straight down to the houses through another kissing gate. Cross over the road and there is a signposted path down to an old railway trackbed and stream. Cross the track and you will see steps down to the footbridge. Go over the bridge and climb up the bank slightly to the left and then proceed to the lower of the two stiles before you.

Follow the very clear path leading through the woods, checked only by occasional stiles. This path eventually emerges onto a wider track before a group of allotments. Your way ahead is between ailing corrugated huts and decaying drystone walls. This meets another path before the end of a row of terraces. Walk up to the road, turn left and then right for the centre of Bargoed and the station. You can actually see the station below.

When you think of the valleys as chapel and foundries and mines it comes as a surprise to find such an uninhabited and green land nearby. This is as much part of the cultural heritage of the valleys as the communi.es themselves, offering as in earlier times breathing space - in more ways than one - for those with an inclination to clear their lungs and minds of stress and toil.

Walk 18: Afan Argoed

Landranger Map: Sheet 170.

Pathfinder Maps: Sheets 1127, 1146 (SS89/99 and SS69/79).

Starting Station: Port Talbot.

Finishing Station: Neath (B.R. Table 125).

Distance: 16 miles (26 km).

Time Required: 8 hours.

Grade: Strenuous. (Easy to Afan Argoed for return bus).

Possible Cut-off Point: Afan Argoed Country Park 6 miles (10 km). Hourly bus service back to Port Talbot along A4107 (South Wales Transport service 232).

Terrain: Mainly lanes and woodland tracks. Several prolonged climbs.

Refreshment and Accommodation: Choice of facilities in Port Talbot and Neath. The nearest Youth Hostel is at Llwynypia in the Rhondda valley.

Tourist Information: Aberdulais Basin, near Neath, West Glamorgan, SA10 8EO. Tel: (0639) 53531.

THE RAIL JOURNEY

The journey to Port Talbot from Cardiff goes through the pleasant Vale of Glamorgan with a stop at Bridgend at its western end. The Llynfi, Ogmore and Garw rivers meet here and flow to the sea guarded by the remains of Norman castles downstream on the Ogmore. Nearby is the resort of Porthcawl, a popular South Wales seaside resort.

Port Talbot

The train passes by the major steel works at Margam before reaching Port Talbot which has grown up alongside the older settlement of Aberavon. The scale of the industry dominates but do not let this dissuade you from this walk for within a mile or so inland the tracks and paths pass through quiet farming countryside into one of the narrowest and most beautiful of the South Wales valleys - Afon Afan.

THE WALK

This walk combines some suprisingly fine South Wales countryside with areas of industrial heritage; areas where nature and commercial afforestation has reclaimed an industrial landscape to make attractive countryside, rich in interest.

The walk can be conveniently divided into two parts; a first section from Port Talbot to Afan Argoed Country Park (6 miles) from where an hourly bus can be caught back to Port Talbot and a second section from Afan Argoed over the hills to Neath.

On leaving the station you come immediately to the roundabout. Cross over and turn right walking along the main A48 road. Pass the Plaza cinema and opposite the Central Garage turn left into Broad St. Pass the school and then turn right into George St. Go left at the next junction and follow the footpath underneath the motorway. Once on the other side turn left into Tan y Groes Street, the A4107, walk around the corner and go right down a road signed to Broom Hill. Turn right before the modern housing. The quiet tarmac lane begins to climb up and away from the seaport, which can now be seen quite clearly.

Mynydd Emroch

Eventually the lane gives way to a rough track by a house and heads towards the forested Mynydd Emroch to your left. The track continues along the edge of the forest and then drops into pastureland, once again curving to the left then to the right. It would be tempting to follow this but at this point you take the lower and less distinct track which bends to the left and becomes a sunken lane. This subsequently bears right and leads down to the main B 4282 road.

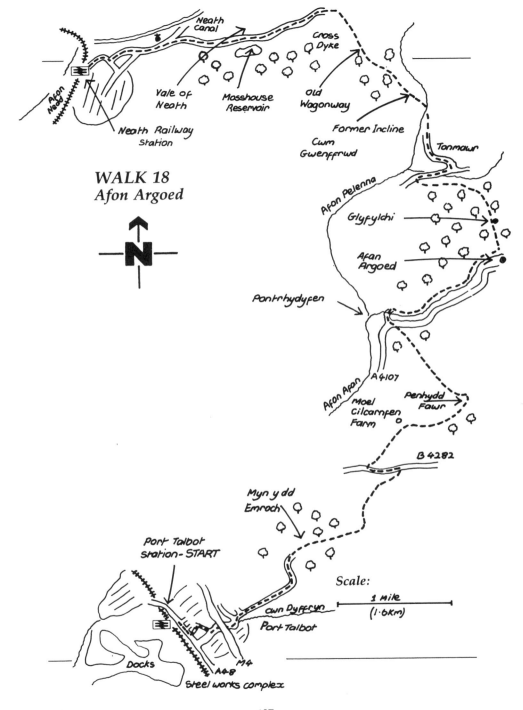

WALK 18
Afon Argoed

Neath Canal

Cross Dyke

Old Wagonway

Vale of Neath

Masshouse Reservoir

Afon Nedd

Neath Railway Station

Former Incline

Cwm Gwenffrwd

Tonmawr

Afon Pelenna

Glyfylchi

Afan Argoed

Pontrhydyfen

A 4107

Afon Afan

Moel Cilcarnfen Farm

Penhydd Fawr

B 4282

Mynydd Emroch

Port Talbot Station - START

Scale:

1 Mile
(1·6Km)

Cwm Dyffryn

Port Talbot

Docks

M4

A48

Steel works complex

137

Farming Country

Cross the road and turn left. Follow the roadside path around the corner until you come across a tarmac lane heading steeply uphill to the right. As the path indicated on the map is not clear on the ground it is best to keep to the lane. As this veers to the left near the brow of the hill you keep ahead with the drystone wall to your right. The farm buildings of Cilcarn come into sight as you rejoin the lane. As this descends and curves right you reach a junction. Turn right here and follow the walled lane until it widens to a boggy triangle with a forest before you. Keep ahead with the wall to your left, going first through a gateway and then continuing up a field, near to the left hand field boundary, until you reach the farmyard of Penhydd Fawr.

With heifers and silage this section can become very muddy so be prepared for slow progress in wet weather. At the crossroads, amid buildings, go left and proceed up this track which soon forks right and leads down by a silage store to woodland. Your path joins a forestry road for a short while and as this bends to the left your track continues ahead and downhill. It eventually zigzags down to the A4107 road.

Pontrhydyfen

Pontrhydyfen, where the rivers Pelenna and Afan meet, is a peaceful hamlet which once had early weaving and other works in the vicinty. It is the birthplace of the actor Richard Burton and the building where he was born is now marked with a plaque.

Cross the road and walk down to the very impressive aqueduct, now dry, which once carried water to local factories. Cross the Afon Afan and then turn right to meet the walkway up the valley. This is a splendid example of the regeneration of a valley after industrialisation. Visitors are surprised by the narrowness and beauty of the valley. This is very much a result of the uplift of land which has meant that the river has cut more deeply into its bed since the Ice Age.

Walk up the left bank of the river until you come to a floodplain used for sporting activivies. The path is well signed and easy to follow. You can see the footbridge ahead. Go up to and cross the bridge if you are going to visit the Afan Argoed Country Park and the Mining Museum. Your way is waymarked by way of the old railway line and underneath the road, then left to the car park and visitor centre.

Afan Argoed Country Park

The Park was designated in 1972 and since those early days there has been a build up of facilities to make a day outing feasible. There is a Visitor Centre providing information. The Welsh Miners' Museum has a simulated coal face, as well as equipment and exhibitions portraying the life of a miner and his family throughout the decades until the closure of the last local pit at Glyncorrwg in 1970. The Museum is open daily from April until October but only at weekends in the winter months. Refreshment facilities are available. On the disused railway line near to the old Cynon Halt is a Cycle Hire centre and the Park is full of nature trails and places to picnic.

Afan Argoed Country Park

You can end the walk here (6 miles) before catching the local bus back to Port Talbot. If such a suggestion sounds too tame and you're ready for the next ten miles, then make your way back to the footbridge for the next part of the walk to Neath.

Michaelston Forest

From the footbridge climb up into the forest, avoiding the first right which is a riverside walk. Go right at the next junction and then next left (if you miss this one go left at the next turning). This brings you by the disused Glyfylchi railway tunnel entrance on the right. This railway, part of the South Wales Mineral Railway, was built mainly to serve the nearby Glyncorrwg colliery. The tunnel, engineered by Isambard Kingdom Brunel himself, was a difficult one to complete but was eventually opened in 1863. It officially only carried coal and freight but occasionally carried miners and their families in empty trucks on special excursions.

Glyfylchi Chapel

Follow the path up until it meets another main track, waymarked, climbing up up from the valley bottom. Go right and follow it up to Glyfylchi chapel, an early chapel, now in ruins. You now come across the Pelenna Mountain Centre. Continue ahead and down a forestry track for about a mile, with the centre to your right. You will see the Pelenna river to your right and also the village of Tonmawr. As you approach the houses there is a track off to the right down to the community centre. Most ramblers use this link path to avoid a circuitous route further down the valley. You come to the road where you turn right.

Tonmawr

Tonmawr is perhaps typical of villages in these parts which once were dominated by coal mining and now have little left to show for two centuries of intensive industry apart from memories, a good rugby pitch and a deep pride. Turn right and walk up the road. Beyond the school you will see steps up to the left. Follow them up to the road once again where you turn left. This road becomes a track and soon you will reach a fork. Go left, crossing the stream and then climbing steeply. It is startling to think that this was once a tramroad and the entire valley a bustle of activity. It seems so still now, but it's not difficult to imagine the sweat, joy and sorrow of the miners who worked the deep underground seams. As you walking past the remains and relics of a once mighty industry you begin to understand something of the hardship and comradeship which made the pit villages of the Welsh valleys.

The track levels in the forest and bears right. Be careful not to miss an inclined path which crosses yours, for at this point you join it and bear left up to a stile and then upwards again onto open pasture.

Parson's Folly Tramroad

Bear right and follow the remains of the wagonway along the top of the valley to a viaduct and through a cutting, the scenery being marred only by wrecked cars. The tramroad was built in the late 1830s by Charles Strange and Robert Parsons to carry coal from local pits to the Neath canal basin at Aberdulais. The line is full of steep inclines and was superseded by the Mineral Railway mentioned earlier. The track passes by a pool and then descends to meet a tarmac lane. There you turn right and pass by the remains of the wagonway and tip .

Returning to Neath

The remainder of the walk is along a quiet lane into the suburbs of Neath. There are good views of the Neath Valley and Swansea Bay. After a short distance you pass by Mosshouse Wood Reservoir built in 1889 to supply Neath with water. Then the lane winds its way down for well over a mile to the main B4434 with views across the Vale of Neath with the Afon Nedd and Neath Canal. Built in the 1820s the Neath and Tennant Canal system played a crucial role in the development of the valley. But railway and eventually road competition became too much for the canal which finally fell into disuse and disrepair in the 1930s.

Neath

Turn left along the B4434 before turning right as the main road veers left for a shorter and more direct road into the town centre and Neath railway station. This compact town which grew up close to the lowest crossing point of the Afon Nedd, has both a Castle and a 12th century Cistercian Abbey. These well-restored monuments are, however, unfortunately sandwiched between modern development - major roads and industry - making it difficult to imagine them as they were in their original setting.

Several attractions in and around the Vale of Neath are worth a visit if you have time, such as the beautifully restored canal basin at Aberdulais and the nearby Penscynor Wildlife Park as well as the Cefn Coed Coal and Steam Centre at Creunant.

Walk 19: *Sugar Loaf*

Landranger Map: Sheet 161.

Outdoor Leisure Map: Sheet 13 Brecon Beacons-Eastern Area.

Starting and Finishing Station: Abergavenny (B.R. Table 87).

Distance: $8^1/2$ miles (13km).

Time Required: Allow 6 hours.

Grade: Strenuous.

Possible Cut-off Point: Llanwenarth after 2 miles of riverside walking.

Terrain: Level paths but some steep climbs throughout.

Refreshment and Accommodation: Plentiful supply in Abergavenny.

Tourist Information: 2 Lower Monk Street, Abergavenny, Gwent NP7 5NA. Tel: (0873) 3254/ 77588.

THE RAIL JOURNEY

The Welsh Marches - or border country - has had a stormy history which now seems hardly credible given the quiet beauty and rural charm of the countryside and the many towns of Shropshire, Herefordshire and Gwent through which the Marches Line (Crewe-Newport-Cardiff) runs; towns of such great charm and character as Shrewsbury, Church Stretton, Ludlow, Leominster, Hereford and Abergavenny.

Abergavenny is now the railhead for Brecon and for the Brecon Beacons National Park. It has a lovely old station built to Great Western specification as are so many of the other stops on the Marches Line.

Abergavenny

The town of Abergavenny sits on a bluff between the Gavenny brook and the River Usk, hence the name. It was originally the site of a Roman fort and in the late 11th century the same site was used to build a castle by the Norman Marcher Lord, Hamelin de Ballon. The ruins are open to the public and date mainly from the 13th and 14th centuries. Situated in the grounds of the castle is Abergavenny Museum. This displays a number of local history exhibits including a Welsh farmhouse kitchen at the turn of the century.

The shopping centre in Abergavenny has been partially pedestrianised and allows the visitor an opportunity to browse at leisure. The town is an ideal location for tours to surrounding places of interest including Tretower Court, Llanvihangel Court, Raglan Castle, and the Big Pit Mining Museum near Blaenavon. They are all served by local buses which start from the bus station, five minutes' walk from the railway station. The Marcher castles of Grosmont, Skenfrith and White Castle are also well worth a visit but there is no regular bus service to this area.

THE WALK

On leaving the station entrance turn left down Station Road and walk to the main A40. Turn right and pass by the Belmont public house. Cross the road and turn left down Mill Close adjacent to a new housing development. This track leads to a kissing gate. Go through it and proceed to the footbridge. Cross this and bear left to the banks of the Usk where you turn right and walk upstream. Cross another footbridge, of smaller dimensions this time, and then continue to walk up-river to the Usk Bridge. There are splendid views of Abergavenny Castle from this section of path.

Usk Bridge

Once at the bridge cross the main A4143 road and to your left are steps back down to the riverside. Follow the clearly defined path upstream. The river curves right and then you cross a tributary stream before proceeding along a level section passing through several fields towards Llanwenarth. You pass by the church a little distance to your right and then come to a junction with a path leading off left and waymarked in red. Do not follow this unless you want to finish the walk here and return to Abergavenny.

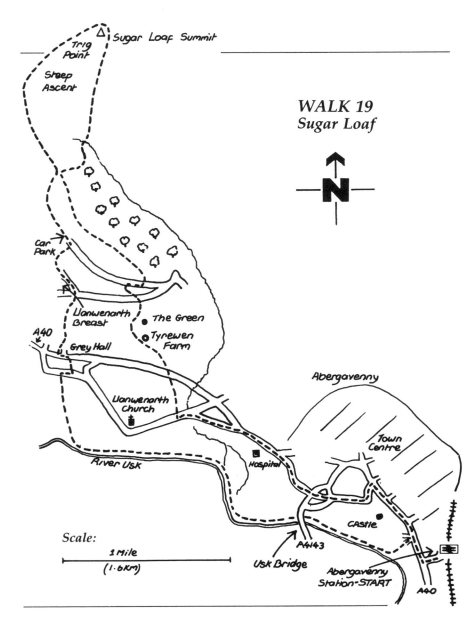

WALK 19
Sugar Loaf

If you are proceeding then continue upstream through this field to another stile. Cross it and bear right but not directly following the hedge to your right. Go through the barred gate ahead and keep the same direction, now with the hedge to your left. Go through the gateway and while the map shows the path heading diagonally right across the field, most ramblers keep ahead to a stile which leads onto a tarmac lane.

Go right for a short distance and you'll see a path leading off through a gateway on the left heading towards Grey Hall on the Brecon Road. The only exit at the other end of the field is a barred gate leading onto the road. Bear left and then cross over. Do not go up the lane by the hall but instead go over the stile by the lane. This leads to the left of the gardens, across a small plot and then along a narrow path to a stile by a stream. Cross them both and continue uphill to a stile ahead. Go over this and now the climbing commences. Skirt the brambles then climb upwards towards the line of power poles, all the time keeping relatively near to the fence on your left. This eventually veers left and you head off right towards what looks like a scout or guide hut. Go over the stile in the field boundary, catching your breath before another short climb up a concrete path to a cross roads.

Ancient Tree-Lined Lane

Cross directly to a track, lined with ancient trees, leading upwards and passing two farms on the right. This meets a track coming in from the right before an old cottage on the left and then climbs up to the right and onto moorland. You soon reach a tarmac lane and then turn left for the car park. There is a viewfinder here and also a commemoration to Viscountess Rhondda who dedicated the Sugar Loaf Mountain for public access in 1936.

The Sugar Loaf

Your way up to The Sugar Loaf is signed but as there are so many paths across the moorland it is easy to become confused. Nevertheless, on a clear day you cannot miss your key objective. At the first main junction, with a drystone wall to the left, go right but within a short distance, as the path opens up, take the second green path on your left. Go slightly right at the next junction, proceeding downhill a little at first. At the next junction keep ahead and the path begins to climb gently at first with the remains of a boundary fence to your left. Take your time. This path becomes steeper and then the final very steep climb is made over a rock strewn area up to the summit marked with a trig point at 596 metres or 1,955 feet above sea level.

Spectacular Views

The views across to the Brecon Beacons and over to the Blorenge and The Skirrid are spectacular and ample reward for the hard ascent. It is often windy at the top so unless you are keen to stay awhile walk along the summit edge in an easterly direction, that is with your back to the trig point, and instead of going directly ahead follow a steep and narrow path running down to your right which soon becomes a boulder strewn slope with several paths. They converge again and the main path begins to become a greener swathe and curves gently to the left.

Cross over a main path and continue downhill into a steeper gully with a stream soon appearing on the left. Keep to the right of it here dipping across a smaller tributary coming in from the right. The path climbs up steeply then as it becomes level again you come to a cross roads. Go left on to the main green track, rather than the smaller paths immediateley to your left. Follow this as it descends gently to old mine workings. The path curves slightly left before crossing another track. It then narrows and curves around to the right through the bracken to emerge onto a tarmac road.

Descent to Abergavenny

Bear right and as the road bends to the right turn left down a narrow path through thick bracken to a stile. Cross this and continue downhill to the lane. Cross over and go through the cottage garden path with care. Continue downhill, keeping company with the hedge on your left, and go through a gate in its bottom left-hand corner. Do not turn left in front of the cottage. Bear right through the second gate which leads into an orchard. Swing slightly to the right through the apples and pears to a stile leading into the next field where you turn left and walk down to a track by the farm building. Follow the hairpin bend through the farm buildings and then continue along the track down to the main Brecon Road.

Cross the road, turn right, then cross the stile on the left. Go down the steep slope, cross the ditch and then walk slightly left to a stile. Go through it and walk directly ahead towards the stream where you will find a stile leading out onto the tarmac lane. Bear left and at the next junction turn right up to the main Brecon Road. Turn right and just beyond the hospital turn right again into Union Road. Follow this to the ring road, which is crossed by a footbridge. This leads through a quiet backwater of Abergavenny and at the next junction with the main A4143 cross over and go ahead to the town centre. Turn left for the shops, right for the station.

It seems difficult to believe that barely two hours or so ago you were standing on the towering summit of Sugar Loaf now seen from a distance.

Walk 20: Tintern Abbey

Landranger Map: 162.

Pathfinder Map: Sheet 1131 (ST49/59).

Starting and Finishing Station: Chepstow (B.R. Table 131).

Distance: 12 miles (19 km).

Time Required: 5 to 6 hours.

Grade: Easy to Moderate.

Possible Cut-Off Point: Tintern. Catch a bus back to Chepstow. No Sunday service.

Terrain: Paths across fields and along wooded tracks which are rough in places. Very few steep climbs. Some road walking on the outward section.

Refreshment and Accommodation: Plentiful supply of both in Chepstow and Tintern. There is a youth hostel in Chepstow.

Tourist Information: The Gatehouse, High Street, Chepstow, Gwent NP6 5LH. Tel. (02912) 3772, or Tintern Abbey,Tintern, Gwent, NP6 6TE. Tel. (02918) 431.

THE RAIL JOURNEY

The line from Gloucester to Newport by way of Lydney and Chepstow is underrated in scenic terms. Much of it is lowland grazing pasture bordering the Severn Estuary but as the train approaches the Forest of Dean the landscape becomes more undulating. The views across the Severn are interesting, particularly as there is a strong ebb and flow in this widening estuary. Coming from the Newport direction the train calls at Caldicott, the nearest point to nearby Caldicott Castle and Country Park.

Brunel's Fine Bridge

The finest section on the line must be Brunel's tubular suspension bridge across the River Wye at Chepstow, offering superb views of the castle and the town. The station, also dating from 1852, is also attributed to Brunel and much of it remains intact.

Chepstow

Chepstow, or Cas-Gwent, was first and foremost a market town, hence the Saxon meaning of the name. Not until the Norman Lords of the Marches, William Fitz Osbern in particular, decided to build a garrison did Chepstow have any military significance. This is understandable as the town is situated on a strategically important crossing over the River Wye on a tidal stretch of the river. The Castle stands magnificent and the 2 metres thick Port Wall, built to protect and enclose the settlement, still remains in several places, including the impressive Town Gate above Beaufort Square.

This is a town of character, once the centre of the yew importing trade, used for the making of bows and other instruments, as well as other small scale industries. Yet the town has not been much affected by industrialisation. Most shops and cafes are to be found in and around Beaufort Square which still has a Saturday market.

THE WALK

The fine walk along the Wye Valley links Chepstow to Tintern Abbey using part of Offa's Dyke Long Distance Route and returns along the other side of the river by the Lower Wye Valley Walk enjoying some fine scenery by Tintern Forest and the Forest of Dean and one of Wales' most romantic ruins.

From the station entrance walk ahead to the new relief road passing by a restaurant and the post office. Go under the new road and follow a short link road to the town centre. If you look left you can see the remains of the ancient walls and in particular The Town Gate which served both as a defence in medieval times and a toll house in later centuries. This is where you will find Chepstow's Tourist Information Centre.

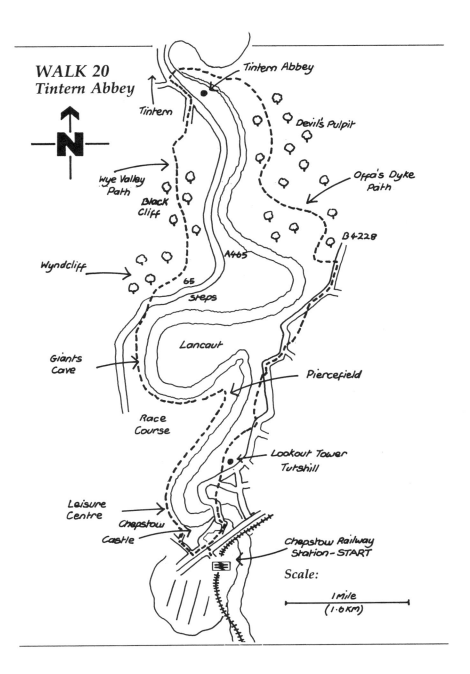

WALK 20
Tintern Abbey

N

Tintern Abbey

Tintern

Devil's Pulpit

Wye Valley Path

Black Cliff

Offa's Dyke Path

A465

B4228

Wyndcliff

65 Steps

Lancaut

Giants Cave

Piercefield

Race Course

Lookout Tower Tutshill

Leisure Centre

Chepstow Castle

Chepstow Railway Station - START

Scale:

1 mile
(1·6 Km)

Rennie's Bridge

Turn right down Bridge Street and proceed to the Castle entrance. The Castle is an essential visit for anyone interested in Marches history but allow sufficient time to enjoy it. On the right hand side of the road is a Stuart Crystal shop and the Chepstow museum. Continue over the magnificent bridge, first engineered by John Rennie in 1816. The size and scale of the Castle can be appreciated from this point. It is also easy to imagine what the river would have looked like in earlier centuries when the port would have been packed with sailing vessels carrying timber, oak bark, wine and other items. The thriving wharves survived well into the nineteenth century until towns across and further down the mouth of the Severn gradually gained ascendancy.

Once over the bridge cross the road and head upwards through a walled passage between houses to Tutshill and across the main A48 road into Moplia road. As this bends to the right go over a stile to your left and head across the field ahead at first then slighly right to its far corner where you cross a stile. Notice the Lookout Tower to the right.

Donkey Track

Keep the wall to your left and go over a stile to the left at its other end. Then proceed right down a short section of drive before crossing a stile on the left leading across a field to another stile. Cross this but do not proceed ahead. Instead turn right to meet the B4428 road. Go left here for a very short section before turning left along a lovely track, thought to have been a donkey lane in earlier times. The path is waymarked past the bungalows. The views of the sea green Wye are magnificent but take care not to go too near the path's steep edge as it is potentially dangerous.

The path emerges onto the road once again and you have to cross over and walk against the traffic for approximately half a mile. The road winds around to the left and your way is on the right along the footpath signposted to Monmouth. Go over the stone stile and within metres you enter a wood where the path turns to the left. On leaving the wood the path crosses a stile and follows the hedge on your right upwards then crosses a series of stiles over a short section leading up to the main B4428 road again. Turn right and walk along the road side once again for about half a mile (1 km). Just before Dennenhill farm cross the road to the stile leading into the woods. This path is also signposted and is well worn. It eventually bears right and then after another level section drops down to the left by way of a series of steps.

The path crosses two sets of access tracks and then swerves right and left along the remains of Offa's Dyke itself. The walk is clear and follows through the woodlands above the Wye for some time. Avoid the lower path to the old railway line but maintain your height until you reach what is known as The Devil's Pulpit, a place where the Devil is supposed to have taunted the monks in the valley below. From here the path begins to descend. You come down to a triangle of tracks and at this point you bear right at first then left, descending once again, avoiding turns to the right to Bigsweir. You come down to the old railway trackbed. Turn right here and cross the railway bridge to the main A466 road. The housing development on the left is centred around one of the old boatyard areas in Tintern, as the river is still tidal at this point.

Tintern

It is hard to believe that Tintern was once an industrial centre, albeit a small one. As early as 1568 there was brass making in the vicinity but in more recent centuries Tintern grew as a centre for making wire. There were also several iron workings with charcoal being produced in the neighbouring Forest of Dean. The railway to Monmouth came in 1876 and though it has been closed for some years, Tintern Station survives as a cafe and local Interpretative Centre. The coming of the railway dramatically reduced the number of sailing vessels on the Wye although pleasure craft could still be chartered in late Victorian times for cruises up and down the river.

Tintern Abbey

Turn left on the road and pass by shops and inns towards the Abbey. This magnificent Cistercian ruin is situated on a broad, grassy bank of the River Wye, surrounded by steep woodland, and was founded in 1131. It was largely rebuilt in the 13th and 14th centuries when the Cistercian Order was amongst the most powerful landowners in the British Isles and flourished until the Dissolution by Henry VIII in 1636.

Tintern Abbey

The Abbey has an important place in literary history, for it was here in 1798 that the Lakeland poet William Wordsworth and his sister Dorothy came on a walking tour which was to result in one of the greatest poems of the Romantic period. This is Wordsworth's "Lines Composed a few miles above Tintern Abbey" which contain descriptions of the landscape "little lines of sporting wood run wild" which are as accurate today as when they were written, as are the reflections on human experience -

"the still sad music of humanity" - made about the time of the French Revolution,which still have a universal significance.

Another visionary figure to visit Tintern was J.M.W. Turner, arguably England's greatest painter, who captured the essence of the romantic ruins in a watercolour of glowing splendour, exhibited at the Royal Academy in 1794, and now in the Victoria & Albert Museum. It is quite remarkable that the major buildings of the Abbey have survived in such good condition despite the removal of the roof all those centuries ago.

Your return journey to Chepstow is almost certainly the way William and Dorothy Wordsworth went in 1798 along what is now known as The Wye Valley Walk, different from the Offa's Dyke path in some respects but nevertheless offering exhilarating views and tranquil corners. Opposite the entrance to the Abbey, turn right into a tarmac lane and turn left at the next junction. This soon becomes a lovely cool woodland track alongside a sparkling stream. Virtually at its head go left and the path climbs up out of the wood to a stile. Cross it and proceed ahead to a stile leading into the wood before you. The path now climbs up through a rougher patch and curves left to level out along Black Cliff and Wyndcliff. There are several quite spectacular views as you progress to the Viewpoint. Turn left down to the 365 steps and descend with caution as some sections are steep.

This leads to the car park below adjacent to the main A466 road. Cross the road and your way is down to the right where a very clear path winds around to a tunnel and then onwards by Giant's Cave. Below you will glimpse the Wye and Waiter's Weir. Further along is the Apostles Rock. The path circles around Piercefield Park, a popular visitor attraction in the 18th century, and continues on to Alcove Wood. Here this glorious, romantic path unceremoniously emerges through urban debris by a modern leisure centre. Such is the twentieth century !

At the main road turn left for the fifteen minute walk into the town centre and railway station.

Walking Notes

Walking Notes

More Country Walking
with quality books from
Sigma Leisure

East Cheshire Walks - *2nd edition* - Graham Beech
Now in its second, enlarged, edition this popular book - with a foreword by David Kitching (Chief Ranger, East Cheshire) - is the essential guide to East Cheshire's great outdoors. With over 200 miles of walks in glorious scenery, a fascinating collection of photographs and helpful sketch maps, this book remains the essential walker's companion for anybody contemplating a walk in East Cheshire. The walks range from 3 to 12 miles and are graded so that anybody can tackle them, from a young family to the serious rambler.
April 1988   ISBN: 1 85058 112 6   £4.95

West Cheshire Walks - Jen Darling
Sub-titled 'Warrington to Whitchurch, Wilmslow to the Wirral', whilst this is yet another of our books of rambles it is definitely not *just* another book. Most of the walks have not been previously published, and here they are described in great detail together with maps, photographs, sketches and notes on the local wild life that will delight both naturalists and casual walkers. Many of the walks are suitable for family outings, though there is a sprinkling of more energetic hikes for the more dedicated rambler.
Summer 1988   ISBN: 1 85058 111 8   £4.95

Staffordshire Walks:simply superb - Les Lumsdon
Containing nearly 30 walks, this offers more than any other Staffordshire walks book. It offers gentle strolls through Staffordshire's pleasant countryside and some of the best hill walking for miles around. There are walks through villages, along canal towpaths and through peaceful woods of this undiscovered haven for walkers. It provides endless ideas for enjoyable days out, places to visit and - most unusual for a book of walks - a good read about the county.
Spring 1988   ISBN: 1 85058 105 3   £4.95

Shropshire Walks - Les Lumsdon
Les captures the charm of Shropshire life - farms, inns and quiet country towns - and leads you on 36 walks throughout the county. Fine hill

walking along Offa's Dyke, The Long Mynd and Caer Caradoc contrast with easy rambles through fields and valleys. Many of the walks are along footpaths rarely used in recent years, and these have been opened up in cooperation with Shropshire County Council.
Summer 1989   ISBN: 1 85058 160 6   £4.95

West Pennine Walks - Mike Cresswell

Written in a lively style, with personal anecdotes, maps and detailed directions, this book contains 32 super walks between 5 and 20 miles that are easily accessible by car or public transport. They are all based in this beautiful and varied area which, although popular with the 'locals', remains undiscovered by many. Unlike many walks books, this one entertains with humour, personal experiences, zest and enthusiasm. It also contains more walks than any other book on the area.
Summer 1988   ISBN:1 85058 093 6   £4.95

Twenty Great Walks from British Rail - Les Lumsdon and Colin Speakman

Here is a unique book that combines the joys of walking with the freedom and enjoyment of travelling by train. No longer do you have to plan circular walks or see the same views twice over - simply use the train and have a great day out! Both authors are well known travel writers, and they travelled and walked every mile described in their book. Detailed sketch maps, directions and information are included.
December 1987   ISBN: 1 85058 099 7   £4.95

South Pennine Escort: - Michael Z. Brooke

Use this book to plan a day out in beautiful & rugged surroundings: hike over the hills (with detailed maps and directions), scramble over the rocks, paddle in the streams, ride a steam railway - or watch colourful customs and explore such picturesque towns as Hebden Bridge, Howarth, Glossop, Stalybridge and Ilkley.
May 1987   ISBN: 1 85058 069 3   £4.95

Sigma Leisure also publish a wide range of town histories for many parts of the North West - please ask for a complete catalogue.

***SIGMA LEISURE* is an imprint of SIGMA PRESS.**
Sigma Press, 1 South Oak Lane, Wilmslow, Cheshire SK9 6AR.
Phone: 0625-531035.